MEMOIRS OF A
SOCCER VAGABOND

Ronald P. Maierhofer

Figure 1
Coach Ron, aged 75

Contact the author care of cornerkickit@gmail.com

First published by Sports Club Management
5722 Whistling Duck Drive
North Myrtle Beach SC, 29582 USA

Library of Congress Card Catalog Number: 1-6358569501
ISBN: 978-069209-302-3

About the Author

Figure 2
Author circa 2016

Author Ron Maierhofer lives in North Myrtle Beach with his wife, Sandra. They share eight children and nineteen grandchildren. He has spent a lifetime in the sport of soccer, playing at youth, club, collegiate, professional, and national team levels. Ron played in nineteen states and forty-two cities in the USA and Canada. He has co-founded soccer entities playing in fourteen states in the USA.

A graduate of Cornell University, Ron was an All-American and inducted into the 1986 Cornell Athletic Hall of Fame in the same class with former U.S. National Soccer Coach Bruce Arena. In 1999, he was inducted into his high school's, The Park School of Buffalo, Athletic Hall of Fame. Ron was a U.S. National Soccer Team Member in 1959. He was the founder and former owner of the Denver Avalanche, of the Major Indoor Soccer League, from 1980 to 1983. Now a sports management consultant and entrepreneur, Ron is the co-founder of Soccer Club Management, LLC, and Sports Club Management, LLC, national soccer training companies providing soccer enrichment and online learning programs to young children under the trade names KinderKickIt, Cornerkick, CornerKickIt, and Touch and Technique.

The author has published over one hundred articles on soccer in community newspapers and magazines. This is his second book. His first book, "*No Money Down, How to Buy a Sports Franchise,*" is about the Denver Avalanche of the Major Indoor Soccer League. Both books can be viewed at www.sportsclubmanagement.org

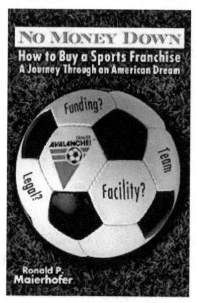

Figure 3 No Money Down

Contents

Preface

Very few of you have heard of me. I'm not Dan Snyder, Ted Turner, or George Steinbrenner. But, I too, owned a professional sports franchise, The Denver Avalanche of the Major Indoor Soccer League. I was also a member of the U.S. National Soccer Team, the dream of every boy and middle-aged man ever kicked a ball. During my soccer journey, I've rubbed shoulders with great players, with Fortune 500 high rollers, politicians and crapshooters, even the real heroes in the world of soccer and sports.

Like the title of a schoolmate's bestseller, "In Search of Excellence," I have strived to achieve my soccer dream and know full well the cost of the pursuit of excellence. I know how fast you have to run to catch the AMERICAN SOCCER DREAM – how sweet it tastes, to chew on it, and how easily it can be snatched away.

No, my name is hardly a household word. I don't make decisions for millions or decide the fate of nations. I am still dreaming at the age of eighty-two and trying to determine my own fate and destiny. And yes, I'm still searching for my next soccer experience. Telling my soccer story is one of my dreams. This is not the memoir of a mover and shaker, reminiscing in his twilight years. Rather, it is a dream realized and presented to all soccer fans by a proud former player, very much involved in the struggle for understanding himself.

This is my story of a working man's lifetime in soccer. I am the son of German immigrants, and I wasn't satisfied with being a butcher—but instead wanted to contribute to the development of soccer in the USA. I played, coached, and started soccer-related businesses. I was fortunate to play without serious injury on youth, high school, college, and professional teams and for the 1959 USA National Soccer Team, which won a bronze medal at the Third Pan-American Games.

Abraham Lincoln once said, "Better to remain silent and thought a fool than to speak out and remove all doubt." My story may not need to be told so much as I need to tell it. But, there are two overriding reasons why you might find my soccer journey interesting – *WE ALL NEED DREAMS, AND YOU COULD EASILY BE ME!*

Acknowledgments

I would like to thank my wife, Sandra Ferony Maierhofer, for her suggestions, tireless support, editing and proofreading of this book. I also offer my deep appreciation to Erin S. Reed for her creativity, editing and insights when creating the front and back covers; to the professional editing of the manuscript by firstediting.com as I prepared the book for its publishing; to the professional formatting by Polgarus Studio; the early encouragement and direction offered by friends, especially Soccer Hall of Famer Len Oliver; a special thanks for the soccer memories created by sons Scott, Jeff, Tim and Craig and finally, a special thank you to our eight children and nineteen grandchildren. They have made us proud.

Chapter 1
History of Soccer/Football
Western New York
1910-1939

Introduction

Several years ago, I was having coffee with Soccer Hall of Fame member Len Oliver at his home in Washington, D.C.

Figure 4
Len Oliver
United States Soccer Hall of Fame

As is usually the case when two old-timers get together, we were reminiscing about our beloved sport and our past experiences over many decades. Len, knowing my background, suggested I write about my lifetime soccer experiences in the many cities and states in which I played and coached. He knew I was born and raised in Buffalo and grew up in a soccer family. Len suggested I first write about my history there and in Western New York. Said

Len, "There are few former players in this country who can say they played on teams spanning eight decades."

I started playing when I was seven years old (1942) and played in league play until the age of sixty-seven (2002), ending up playing in the Men's Over-30 League in the Washington, D.C. metro area. I continued to play in exhibition games until I was seventy-one. Yes, I will shortly be eighty-three years young. I am still a soccer coach and heavily involved in two soccer training and consulting companies that I co-founded, Soccer Club Management, LLC and Sports Club Management, LLC.

Len's encouragement led me to decide to write about soccer in the "good old days." As I moved forward through my early life, high school, college, and business careers, I was fortunate to play, coach, or have soccer business interests in nineteen states. These states include New York, Ohio, Texas, California, Nevada, Colorado, Pennsylvania, Rhode Island, Connecticut, Massachusetts, New Hampshire, New Jersey, Maryland, Minnesota, Indiana, Illinois, Michigan, Wyoming and South Carolina.

I also played in several cities in Canada along the way, including Toronto, Hamilton, Kitchener, London, St. Catherine, Windsor, Fort Erie, Welland, and Niagara Falls. Many of those Canadian teams played in the Ontario Soccer League. The Toronto Belfast United team played in the Eastern Ontario Soccer Association, now the Canadian Professional Soccer League. On reflection, it appears that I could be considered a *soccer vagabond*.

1910 – 1940 Soccer in Western New York

There is limited information about soccer in Western New York from 1910 to 1920. This period included the war years.

Before writing about my decades of soccer, I did some research about soccer in Western NY during the early 1900s and prior to my entry into the sport in 1940. Since I lived in the Washington, D.C. metro area, I researched my dad's claims by reviewing newspaper articles stored in the Library of Congress about early soccer in Western New York. I was shocked to find that soccer flourished in Buffalo as early as 1910.

Buffalo, like many other cities on the east coast, attracted many immigrants in the early 20th century, mostly from Germany and other European countries. It had a growing population mix affectionately called "PIGI," which represented the Polish, Italian, German, and Irish communities. These communities were informally organized by city blocks and each country's immigrants would mostly live within the confines of the community.

I reviewed the microfilmed newspaper articles at the Library of Congress and found the earliest mention of Western NY soccer was in the spring of 1910. This is quite a bit later than the first reported soccer game in the United States being played by the Oneida Club of Boston in 1862.

On a cold, snowy Sunday, April 10, 1910, the Buffalo Rovers played Saint George of Jamestown, kicking off the first game. These teams later became part of the Buffalo District Amateur Soccer League, formed in 1913. The league included the Buffalo Rovers, the Buffalo Rangers, the Saint George of Jamestown, the Buffalo Nomads, and the Niagara Falls Wanderers. The local newspaper, the Buffalo Express, covered the games and faithfully reported each week's matches.

Concurrent with this new Buffalo league, Jamestown, New York, located about seventy-five miles west of Buffalo and primarily a destination city for immigrants from Sweden and Denmark, formed its own league in 1910, called the Jamestown United League. Teams included the McNaughton Rangers from Rochester, NY, a local Jamestown team, Sons of Saint George, the Niagara Falls Rangers, the Colonial Football Club of Niagara Falls and the United Club from Buffalo. The automobile trips to play in Jamestown and Rochester were arduous and often took almost three hours of traveling one way to play.

By 1913, the number of teams playing had grown rapidly, leading to the formation of the Buffalo District Amateur Soccer League. The league boasted eighteen teams, and soccer was thriving. My first club, the Buffalo Beck's, was founded at that time. Buffalo was one of the largest beer producers in the country in this era. There were twenty-nine breweries in Buffalo in 1919 and Magnus Beck's Brewery was one of the largest producers in Buffalo. It continued to support amateur soccer for years and sponsored our soccer club.

1920-1939

The 1920s were widely considered to be the first golden era in American soccer. There was another influx of immigrants again after World War I, primarily from European countries. They brought with them their soccer traditions and the game grew rapidly. The first American Soccer League was established in 1921 by the merger of teams from the Southern New England Soccer League and the National Association Football League.

There were no true national leagues for any of the major sports. Many of you on the east coast probably remember the soccer powerhouses in these two leagues, including Bethlehem Steel, New York F.C., J&P Coates, and Fall River. These teams imported top players from the Scottish and English Leagues and the league was considered one of the strongest in the world. The league shut down in 1933.

By this time, many cities had semi-professional or amateur soccer leagues, including: The National Soccer League of Chicago, with well-known teams like the Chicago Schwaben and the Chicago Kickers; the National Soccer League, from New York; the New Jersey Soccer Association and the St. Louis Soccer League. Most of these teams competed in the National Open Challenge Cup. Buffalo, with a population of 400,000+ in 1922, had over 100,000 German immigrants. Many of these immigrants were also soccer nuts.

Teams playing at this time included the German Athletic Club, Kolping S.C., Germania, Buffalo Amateurs, the Blizzard, the Rovers, the Turners, the Victoria's, and Polonia. These teams from Buffalo and Western New York played many nationally recognized teams during the cup competitions. As an example of its strength, the Niagara Falls McKenzie's, in 1928, lost in the final of the national challenge cup to perennial national champions, Fall River of Massachusetts.

By the 1930s, the Buffalo Amateur Soccer League, the Intercity League of Western New York, and the Niagara Frontier Soccer League were playing a higher level of soccer. My father's club, Germania, was considered by 1932 to be one of the best in Western New York and in amateur soccer. I was shocked as I researched this early period in soccer, including my Dad's claim of a powerhouse team in 1932.

Many of the friends of our family, including Hall of Fame member (1951) Rudy Epperlein, were either on the Germania F.C. or the German A.C. Surprisingly, I found my Dad's claim to be slightly inaccurate and his team did not play in a national quarterfinal match. But it won the league championship in the fall of 1932; and in September, as a cup tune-up, they beat the visiting Brantford City A.C. 4-1. Brantford City was playing in the Canadian National League at the time. On October 17, 1932, the Germania F.C. beat the Rochester Celtics of the Niagara Frontier League to represent Western New York in the National Challenge Cup. The team traveled to Cleveland to play Salvia for the pre-quarterfinal of the National Challenge Cup and lost 4-1. Dad's team never did make it to the quarterfinals.

Figure 5
Germania Soccer Club 1932
Family Photo – Paul Maierhofer 3rd from Left
Eddie Maierhofer 6th from Left

Figure 6
Edward Maierhofer, Circa 1932

bers of the Germania Soccer Club, 1932 national cup finalists in Western
show in this photo from Archie Henderson, 72 Catherine St., Williamsvi
of K. LeBron, at left in second row. L to R, front, are: P. Maierhofer, K
r. Second row: LeBron, H. Wicky, E. Maierhofer. Standing: H. Leiner, C.
er, R. Kober, W. Eisenmann, A. Marshall, E. Sackmann and F. Sackmann (i

Figure 7
Germania Soccer Club 1932
National Cup Finalist WNY
Buffalo Evening News Photo

Chapter 2
World War II on the Field
1940 – 1948

My dad, Edward (Eddie) Maierhofer, emigrated from Rohrbach, Germany (south of Frankfurt) into the United States in 1926 and settled in Buffalo, NY, close to his brother Paul and sister Beulah. He met my mother, Bertha, and they married in 1933. She was eighteen at the time and had emigrated from Düsseldorf, Germany when she was twelve. I was their first child, born in 1935.

Figure 8
Bertha Maierhofer (MOM)

Figure 9
Ron 1935

Europe was going through major inflation after World War I. My father often told stories to us about life in Germany during that period. He was a six-day bicycle and motorcycle racer and a butcher in a traveling circus that toured throughout Europe. He spoke several languages. One tale I vividly remember him sharing was that workers got paid twice a day in the 1920s— once at noon when a wheel barrel of money was enough to buy a pack of cigarettes. They got paid again at the end of the day, when they were paid with two wheel barrels of money, enough to pay for the same pack of cigarettes. Before immigrating to the USA, he owned a specialty retail meat shop in Baden-Baden on the German Riviera.

The European inflation during the 1920s led to one of the largest influxes of Europeans into the USA. The immigration rules were significantly tougher in those days. An immigrant, before being accepted into our country, had to pass a physical, have $200 in cash or assets, have a job waiting, and be sponsored by a citizen.

Dad worked three jobs from the time he arrived in Buffalo from Germany. Many evenings he arrived home from work at two in the morning. He was up at 6 a.m. again and off to work as a butcher in a pig slaughterhouse, where he learned Polish. Later, he worked in an exclusive butcher shop. By 1940, he had accumulated enough money to start his own business, combining a retail meat store with a wholesale meat business and a sausage manufacturing plant.

Figure 10
Maierhofer's Truck 1951
Ron' Accident to the Bumper

Figure 11
Ronnie and Howie 1941

Soccer was an everyday event in our family. In 1942, Dad co-founded the first youth soccer team in Buffalo. The first age group was seven to nine years old. He paid all the expenses for the team, including uniforms, balls, nets, and equipment for the team. The uniforms we wore aptly had the monikers Maierhofer Meats, Maierhofer Hams, and Maierhofer Sausages. Pretty schmaltzy!

Figure 12
Howie and Ron 1942

The team played for the Buffalo Beck's Soccer Club, sponsored by one of the many breweries located in Buffalo at the time. A number of the players on the Buffalo Beck's Team had sons close to my age and they joined the team. Those teammates included Tom Webb, Ron Schultz, Dean Eisenman, Billie Stutz, and his brother Danny Stutz.

Figure 13
Our Soccer Team 1948
The Old Swimming Hole
Ron and Howie in the Center Front Row

Soon, kids whose fathers played for immigrant-based teams like Polonia (Polish) Britannia (British), Italia (Italian), Rochester Ukrainians, and others, were formed. There was no formal league or youth soccer association. Youth soccer was to become organized in Buffalo around 1949 by Albert Odenbach, who was associated with Club Germania. We traveled with the senior teams to the cities in which they competed. Those cities included Niagara Falls, Rochester, Syracuse, Detroit, Chicago, Cleveland, and Jamestown. They also traveled to Canadian cities like Toronto, Hamilton, Kitchener, Niagara Falls, and London.

World War II in Europe was heating up in 1941. Although the war began with Nazi Germany's attack on Poland in September 1939, the United States did not enter the war until after the Japanese bombed the American fleet in Pearl Harbor, Hawaii, on December 7, 1941. Four days later, December 11, 1941, Germany declared war on the United States.

Life and soccer life as we knew it changed. Few of you probably remember the blackouts, internment, and ration stamps. Food, gas, and other staples were in short supply. My father's business boomed in 1941. There would be lines three blocks long waiting to get into his retail store, with policemen managing the line. Often, my father would travel to the farms surrounding Buffalo to acquire meat products for his business. Customers buying from my dad had to have ration cards and stamps. Gas was hard to find; it sold for twelve cents a gallon and required gas stamps. Cigarette smokers saved the aluminum foil in their pack of cigarettes and turned it into schools holding drives to help the war effort.

I remember paper drives at our elementary school to help the war effort. My brother Howie and I would scrounge paper and metal and transport it to the school where it was weighed for the contest. Howie and I usually won the competition.

Soccer was the main recreation for the hard-working immigrants during those years. Most worked six days a week. Sundays were set aside for church, soccer and family meals. Each nationality had a first, reserve, and youth team. Being of German descent was not easy during these years. Each nationality team would take out their personal feeling about the war on the soccer pitch. Each game felt like you were in a World War II battle.

To this day, I have the scars to prove it. Yet, once the game ended, everybody went to the home team's clubhouse. There, they ate, drank, danced, and sang together. They were no longer Italian, German, Polish, British, or Ukrainian immigrants. Rather, they were Americans and proud of it. It was a wonderful exposure to the immigrants who helped our country be one of the world's best societies in which to live.

Early Training

Today's coaches would have difficulty agreeing that the training system in those early days could produce great players. The current coaching license system was not in existence. Most players growing up in this period learned by example. They watched their fathers or relatives play and tried to emulate them on the field when they played. Older players passed down their knowledge and training routine, if any, to the younger players.

My father's meat business building had three floors and a basement. Our family lived on the second floor. The building was made of brick and was about 200 feet long, with two doors with windows. Our father provided leather balls, which had to be constantly repaired and had a rubber innertube. The official repairer of the balls was Hall of Famer, Rudy Epperlein, who played on my father's team and lived close by.

Our Germanic father suggested that we hit a ball against the brick wall one thousand times a day before we could go out and play. Many times, we broke the glass windows in the doors. Dad never said anything and just repaired the broken windows. Luckily, Howie and I could practice together and devised a lot of games using handball rules. It really helped in developing our ball skills.

We were required to work in the family business from the age of seven. By ten years of age, our weightlifting training consisted of lifting hind-quarters and fore-quarters of cows, hundreds of times a day. A hind-quarter averaged 138 pounds and a fore-quarter averaged about 225 pounds. That was a lot of weight to be lifting for young 10-13-year-old kids. To strengthen our legs, we would carry each other on our backs, fireman style. By the time we were high school age, our bodies were far more powerful than most children. Yet, we were no different than many other children of immigrants. Their fathers worked at hard, demanding jobs—bricklayers, masons, carpenters, painters, firemen, laborers, pipefitters, plumbers, and construction workers to name a few.

Our coach, Rudy Epperlein, focused on team play, moving the ball, and moving off the ball. Your physical conditioning was expected when you walked on the field. I was named to the U.S. National Soccer Team in 1959. I doubt if I could juggle the ball twenty times. My thirteen-year-old son, Jeff Maierhofer, juggled the ball 9600 times, which included 3600 times using his head—quite a difference in skill development emphasis. Having said that, today's players are bigger, stronger, smarter, and considerably more skilled. The development of qualified coaching over the years has also significantly raised the level of play.

I continued to play through the 1940s. We played in the informal youth league until 1949 as the Maierhofer Meats Team. By 1949, everyone on the team, except me, was getting bigger and stronger. I was still the smallest member of the team.

Figure 14
Maierhofer Meat's Youth Team 1949
Ron kneeling to goalie's left arm

The Buffalo Becks Soccer Club had a Reserve Team. Howie and I were added to the team in 1950. I was fifteen years old. Norm Weidner, who was to become an All-American at Buffalo State (now SUNY Buffalo) and is in its Soccer Hall of Fame, was on that reserve team, as was Eddie Maierhofer Abrahams, my cousin. Also on the team was Art Meyer who was a teacher at the Park School of Buffalo. We won the Western New York Reserve Division Championships in 1951 and 1952.

Figure 15
Buffalo Becks Reserve Soccer Team
Champions 1951
Ron kneeling 2ⁿᵈ from the left

When the Touring Germans came to Buffalo – 1951

There was a memorable event on May 13, 1951. The Buffalo Beck's Soccer Club, made up of mostly German-Americans, sponsored a game with the highly ranked Eintracht Frankfurt Futball Team, then playing in the Oberliga Süd, a predecessor to the German Bundesliga. Rudy Epperlein headed up the committee to bring the German team to the U.S.A. Rudy had been associated with the Beck's team for many years and later that year he was elected to the U.S. Soccer Hall of Fame.

Figure 16
Eintracht Frankfurt Futball Team Logo
Now a Member of the German Bundesliga

My father was Chairman of the Sponsorship/Advertising Committee for the game. The Beck's were the defending Western New York soccer champions. Even though I was playing on the Beck's reserve team, Rudy selected me to join the team and play. I was 16 years old at the time. The game was under the lights and 35,000 fans attended. The Beck's lost thirteen to one.

Figure 17
Ron, May 14, 1951
Eintracht Frankfurt vs Becks -13-1 Eintracht

A blog on March 9, 2014 about the 1951 game was compiled by the *Upper90* (Western New York's Soccer Magazine):

Over the last few weeks, you may have noticed some major professional clubs from around the world visiting the United States on a preseason tour. The biggest names in the game have made a point to come across the pond to market themselves to the burgeoning American soccer crowd and make some quick cash as they prepare for their upcoming seasons.

Premier League giants Manchester United, Tottenham Hotspur, Manchester City and Arsenal have all faced MLS clubs, as will German power Bayern Munich in the upcoming MLS All-Star Game. Even smaller EPL clubs like Swansea City have made the trip, with the Swans' including a loss to Minnesota United of the NASL. It's a sign of the strength and the allure of the growing passion for soccer here. But it isn't new. And it's something that has a history in western New York.

Back in 1951, several clubs made the trip to North America for a summer tour. The diverse collection of clubs included England's Fulham, AIK of Stockholm, Sweden, Scotland's Glasgow Celtic and Eintracht Frankfurt of Germany.

In January of that year, the local German-American club here in Buffalo revealed plans that they were working to bring Eintracht to Buffalo. The game was set for Friday, May 11, 1951 at Civic Stadium in Buffalo (which would be renamed War Memorial Stadium in 1960), and pit the visiting Germans against a team of Western New York All-Stars sponsored by the Magnus Beck Brewery Company.

The local team was a compilation of the best players in the area. The squad featured Rudy Epperlein, a center midfielder for the Beck's club team who that year was named to the National Soccer Hall of Fame. They would play a few warm-up matches against some Canadian major league clubs as a tune-up for the big game. A few warmup matches wouldn't be quite enough.

Eintracht finished the 1950-51 placing 8th of 18 teams in Oberliga Süd, one spot ahead of a little club known as Bayern Munich. Prior to the Bundesliga's formation in 1963, German clubs participated in regional leagues. The Frankfurters were hardly remarkable at that point, but were trending upward. Their American tour would give them a good experience, as well as some good results.

Five days prior to their Buffalo visit, Eintracht faced the German American League stars at Randall's Island, New York. The visitors from Frankfurt rolled to a 5-2 victory and headed off to the Queen City. The game itself was not close.

In front of 3,500 fans on a wet night inside Civic Stadium, where capacity was north of 35,000, the touring Germans put on a show. Eintracht forward Alfred Kraus scored in the third minute to open the scoring. Then he scored again in the fifth minute. Then teammate Kurt Krömmelbein made it a three-goal margin in the seventh, only to have Kraus score again. Eight minutes in, it was Eintracht 4, Beck's 0. That was about as close as it would ever be.

The Frankfurt club would lead 7-0 at halftime, and took the match by a 13-1 final. Buffalo's squad would have a lone bright moment, as Hans Felgemacher would break the clean sheet in the 71st minute, beating Eintracht keeper Helmuth Henig. But they did lose. 13-1. Kraus would tally seven goals, Hubert Schieth and Alfred Pfaff scored twice, while Krömmelbein and Joachim Jänisch each netted one. After the match, Eintracht Frankfurt continued their tour, dropping the Toledo Turners by a 5-1 score in Ohio just two days later. They visited St. Louis and Milwaukee as well, before returning to the New York area and playing three more matches there.

Overall, they would win six of their eight games, only losing to Zenthoefers in St. Louis and Glasgow Celtic, on a tour themselves, in Randalls Island. Despite the mid-table finish in 1951, there were great things ahead for Frankfurt. Eintracht would finish 4th in the league in 1951-52 and claiming the league title in 1953. They'd win their Oberliga and the German championship in 1959, and joined the Bundesliga in 1963.

Currently, they'd be best known for featuring United States men's national team winger/back Timothy Chandler. For Buffalo, it would be a rare glimpse at the world's best. Touring European teams have criss-crossed the nation on a yearly basis, but other than a 1977 visit from famed Italian club S.S. Lazio, the Western New York region has frequently been passed over.

As the game grows in the United States, that may change. But until then, there will always be that rainy night at Civic Stadium.

Figure 18
Hans (John) Felgemacher and Family
Beck's Goal Scorer vs Eintracht Frankfurt, May 11, 1951
Felgemachermasonry.com website

Chapter 3
Parkin' in High School and O Canada!
1949 – 1955

My life and my dreams changed significantly in 1951. One evening at soccer practice with the Buffalo Beck's reserve team, I was approached by Jackie Knopp, who was playing on the Beck's first division team. Jackie mentioned that he was a teacher and the varsity soccer coach at a private school named The Park School of Buffalo. He asked if I would be interested in attending the Park School as a student and playing soccer.

The Park School was one of the two private schools in the Buffalo metropolitan area at the time and it had an excellent soccer program. However, it was very expensive and I doubted my parents could or would finance the cost of attendance there. Jackie had said he thought I would be awarded an athletic scholarship if I showed interest. I was excited about the prospect and convinced my parents that I wanted to attend Park School. There would be little cost since it had offered me the scholarship. My parents were uneducated, neither of which had finished high school. They had difficulty in understanding the opportunity of a better education but reluctantly agreed to allow me to take advantage of the offer. Little did I know at that time that this decision was to change my life forever.

I accepted the offer to attend Park School, subject to taking its entrance exams. The school administrators told me that colleges accepted 100% of its graduates. There were several tests, including an IQ test and I recollect it was very difficult. I must have passed it since the school accepted me. Luckily, Jackie Knopp was my math teacher and was of considerable help to me academically while a student there. The school was far more challenging than what I was used to. As an example, in order to graduate, a thesis had to be completed in the English class. My thesis was on President Teddy Roosevelt's Conservation Policy. It was seventy-four typewritten pages and my research bibliography was over one hundred source books.

I started Park School in the fall of 1951 and graduated in June of 1953. While at school, I participated in five varsity sports: soccer, wrestling, basketball, baseball, and track. Jackie Knopp was my coach for soccer but the other four sports I played were coached by Coach Herb Mols. Coach Mols strongly believed participating in a variety of sports helps you become a better athlete.

I received several honors while playing athletics at Park School, including the captain of its soccer teams in 1951 and 1952. Park School played in the Conference of Upstate Private Schools and I was selected for its All-Star Soccer Teams in those years. Park School inducted me into its Athletic Hall of Fame in 1999.

Figure 19
Park School Athletic Hall of Fame,
Ron, Jackie Knopp and Howie
1999

Coach Mols of Park School of Buffalo was the singular most influential person in my athletic lifetime. Much of the foundation of my character and success in life I owe to him. Coach Mols exemplified the good qualities we all would like to see in our coaches and leaders. He was a winner on and off the field and represented the true meaning of sportsmanship. He always taught his players to win with class and if they didn't win, to show that same class in defeat. He always played by the rules, leading by example and demonstrating that winning isn't everything.

As I reflected on what to say about this extraordinary man, I found myself looking inwardly. As I see it, in order to measure the influence of anyone on one's life, you first have to look at the results of that influence. My parents embodied the American dream and I was raised in that environment. Coach Mols then added to my parents' influence, convincing me, no, insisting that I participate in other varsity sports at Park. By the end of my senior year, I had played varsity soccer, basketball, wrestling, baseball, and track, with some success. Later, I played soccer and lacrosse at Cornell University and was later elected to its Athletic Hall of Fame.

One memory in particular stands out that shows the measure and influence of Coach Mols on one's life. It was 1953 and the spring of my senior year at Park School. It was three weeks from graduation and we had finished the spring athletic seasons. On a rainy day, the senior class president (one of our outstanding athletes) and I (the senior class vice president), decided to skip required "athletics" and go to a movie in downtown Buffalo.

We had senior privileges to go off campus and my accomplice had an automobile. When we returned to school the next morning, Coach Mols met with us. He pointed out that we were supposed to be role models for the other students. We had been captains or co-captains of several of the sports led by Coach Mols. On the spot, Coach Mols, in spite of it being an unpopular decision, suspended us from school as an example of what happens when one breaks the rules. The class president had to work forty hours in order to return to school (his choice of punishment) to graduate. I had to write a lengthy report (my choice) in order to be allowed to return to school. Once again, Coach Mols demonstrated his evenness in leadership, not allowing "favorite sons" to get favorite treatment.

As I reflect on this episode in my life, and the harshness of Coach Mols' discipline, sixty-five years later, I understand the strength of his leadership and mentoring. He taught me to be steadfast in applying one's values to everyday life and to live with the consequences. Before attending Cornell, I was drafted into the 101st Airborne. The greatest tribute I can bestow upon Coach Mols is a powerful belief that if I were to be taking a hill, I would want him at my side. It is also my belief that his most outstanding successes were helping build the character of the young people by whom he was surrounded. It was not just the athletic accolades that separate this man from the rest.

1953-1955 Playing in Canada

The Beck's played a number of Canadian teams during the early 1950s. Usually, our team would leave early Sunday morning during the off-season, play the game in the afternoon, party a little at the home team's club, and then drive back to Buffalo later that evening. Most of the teams were located in the province of Ontario, Canada and included Niagara Falls, Hamilton, Windsor, Welland, London, Toronto, Ottawa, St. Catharines, Kitchener, and Toronto.

The most notable games were in Kitchener and Toronto in 1954. My brother Howie and I were staying alone that weekend. Our parents had scheduled a long weekend in Cleveland. Howie and I were left to oversee the family business. Early Sunday morning, the team left to play in Kitchener. The team had arranged for a small bus to transport players and family. A few of us drove in our cars. Howie decided to travel on the bus and I drove with teammates.

We arrived in Kitchener and played the game. After the game, the Kitchener team invited us to its club to party. The party was organized like a high school dance. The ladies were all sitting on chairs around the wall. When the music started, the men would saunter over, pick a dance partner, and ask a lady to dance. After the dance, the lady would return to her chair. All very proper.

Later, the teammates I had driven to Kitchener with said they were ready to drive back to Buffalo. Howie had driven there on the bus. We arrived back at our clubhouse and the bus arrived a little later. Howie was not on the bus. We had no cell phones in those days so it was impossible to contact him. The next day, he arrived home and said he just lost track of time and just missed the bus. The last I had seen him was in the Kitchener team's clubhouse, dancing with a young teacher. We never shared that weekend with our parents and I never did find out how he returned to Buffalo.

Late summer 1954, Howie and I were contacted by a Toronto team in the Eastern Ontario Professional Soccer League. It was called Belfast United and they were looking for a few American players. They said they would like to sign us for the season, which started in the fall and that they played games on Wednesday and Saturday. They indicated we were recommended by Rudy Epperlein.

The U.S Olympic Soccer Team was made up of amateur players at the time and Howie and I wanted to maintain our amateur status. Today, the U.S. Olympic Team is made up of U22 players, which can be pros or amateurs. We made the team aware of our concerns and they came back with a proposal. Its sponsor was Molson's Ale, a Canadian brewery. Molson's, at that time, was not available in the USA. They offered to gift us a case of Molson's Ale for each game. The USA Customs at the Peace Bridge allowed a case of Molson's for each twenty-four-hour block one stayed in Canada. Howie and I frequently pulled off the road back to Buffalo and slept in our car. Oh, how times have changed!

Chapter 4
Long Trip to Long Island
1955 – 1957

These years marked a major change in my life. By 1954, I had transferred from the Buffalo Business School to Canisius College in Buffalo. I was taking evening courses, including accounting, logic, philosophy, cosmology (the study of the universe) and epistemology (the study of knowledge). I had also signed up for the Air Force National Guard to be a jet pilot. I had passed the physical and mental requirements and was awaiting assignment to the Air Force Pilot Training School at Waco Air Force Base in Texas. My first airplane ride ever was in an F-94 All Weather Jet. It had two seats—one for the pilot and one for the Navigator.

The USA was still at war with North Korea in 1954. The USA had a draft system for supplying troops for the effort. Fortunately for me, the Korean War Armistice ended the war in 1954. But, the Draft was still being used in 1955 and our draft numbers were drawn for my brother Howie and me. Howie had flat feet and was found not eligible to be drafted. I, however, was drafted in October 1954 and assigned to basic training with the 101st Airborne at Fort Jackson, Columbia, SC. I had no way of knowing that when I returned to South Carolina in 2014, I would have my own soccer training company.

I did not have time to play soccer during my basic training, which ended three months later. I was assigned to the Army Missile Command at Fort Slocum, NY. Fort Slocum was on a small island in the Long Island Sound. To get to it, you had to take a ferry service out of New Rochelle. The command center was at Fort Slocum, but the actual Nike Missile Delivery

System was located on another island a mile away called Hart Island. The Army's Chaplain's School and the Army Information School were also located on Fort Slocum.

Figure 20
Ron Maierhofer
Soldier of the Month 1955
101st Airborne – Fort Jackson, SC

Early in 1954, my cousin, Edward Maierhofer Abrams, moved from Buffalo to Massapequa Park, NY and became the Principal of the Massapequa Park High School. He was joined at the high school by his close friend Norm Weidner. Norm was a teammate of mine with the Buffalo Beck's Reserve Team. Norm graduated from Buffalo State Teacher's College (now SUNY of Buffalo) in 1953 and was its head coach of Men's Soccer in the fall of 1953. Norm had asked me to assist in coaching that team. Norm was inducted into the SUNY Buffalo Athletic Hall of Fame in 1989. He played four years (1948-1953) as a forward for Buffalo State. He was named to the All New York State Soccer Team three times during his career at Buffalo State and also to the Collegiate All-American Team in 1953.

Figure 21
Norm Weidner SUNY Buffalo
Athletic Hall of Fame 1989

When I arrived at Fort Slocum, I called Norm at his Massapequa Park phone number. He indicated that he and Eddie were playing for Huntington Sports Club in the Long Island Soccer Football Major League. The Long Island Soccer Football Major League, in addition to the Huntington Sports Club, included Hempstead S.C., Massapequa S.C., Lindenhurst Sports Club, Glen Cove S.C., Mineola S.C., Sea Cliff F.C., Great Neck Wonders, Flushing Heights S.C. and Franklyn Square S.C. Sea Cliff F.C. won the Major League Championship in 1955 and Lindenhurst Sports Club won it in 1956 and 1957. I graciously accepted their offer to play with them on the Huntington Sports Club Team.

I did not understand the difficulty of playing with them on that team in 1955-1957. I had a four-hour trip, one way, to play a game on Long Island. Each Sunday, I first took the ferry from Fort Slocum to New Rochelle. I then took a cab to the New Rochelle train station, which I traveled on to Grand Central Station. I took the subway from Grand Central Station to the Airline Terminal and connected with the Long Island train. I would arrive by train, close to the city in which we were playing. Sometimes, either Norm or Eddie would pick me up and take me to the field, or, I would take a cab to the field. I would then play the game, have a few beers and dance a little in the hosting team's clubhouse and then take a cab or hitch a ride with someone to the train station. I took another four-hour trip back to Fort Slocum, often arriving between midnight and reveille at the barracks. Thus the long trip to Long Island.

indy, Mineola Keep Deadloc

Lindenhurst and Mineola remained tied for the Long Island Soccer League lead yesterday, Lindy ripping Patchogue, 5-1, and Mineola blanking Franklin Square 2-0. They have 21 points each on 10 wins and a tie, but Lindenhurst has lost only one to three setbacks for the County Seaters.

Martin Bopp had two goals and two assists for Lindenhurst while Tom Tracy added two goals and Art Lesburg tallied once. Valente Kurz saved Patchogue from a shutout.

Jamie Corrica and Paul Vass hit the nets for Mineola on passes from Ewe Knudsen and Arturo Saraiva.

In other senior action, Airlines beat Freeport, 4-2; Sea Cliff nipped Huntington, 4-3; Glen Cove topped Grumman, 3-2; and Great Neck was routed in a National Amateur Cup game by Maritimo of New Jersey, 8-0.

Frank Graham had two goals and two assists for the Airlines with Rea Sacks getting one tally and two assists. Dan Smith scored twice for Freeport . . . Henry Purcell's goal broke a 3-3 tie for Sea Cliff whose other scores were by Rudy Beck, Don Loughran and Art Othen, Dan Schmidt (twice) and Ron Maershoser were Huntington scorers . . .

Figure 22
Game with Huntington 1956
"Maierhoser" Scored a Goal
Long Island Times

During this time, I would occasionally play for the Simon Pure's team, especially when they played in the US Open or Amateur Cup. Those games were played after the fall soccer season and in the dead of winter. It was not unusual to play in a snowstorm in Buffalo.

The New York State Thruway partially opened up in 1954. It was fully completed in August of 1956. I would take a cab from Fort Slocum to the Bronx. The cab would drop me off at the entrance to the Thruway. I would then hitchhike from the Bronx to Buffalo to play a game with the Simon's. After the game, I would hitchhike back to Fort Slocum. The trip was about 450 miles and most times it took me twelve hours to make the trip one way. Crazy! It was not unusual to occasionally slide off the Thruway during a snowstorm hitchhiking with one of the drivers who picked me up. Hitchhiking wasn't unusual back then, though it certainly isn't safe in this day and age!

I remember playing one such game in Syracuse. It was a dreary weekend and I was to meet the team in Syracuse. We played the Syracuse Italians and its field was surrounded by home team fans watching the game. During the game, a cross from our right wing (striker) came into the penalty box. I went up in the air to head it and collided with the goalkeeper, who went down. Quickly, the playing field was filled with irate Syracuse fans. Players and fans began fighting. Suddenly, a fan spit at me from my side. I did not hesitate and turned and hit the fan who spit on me. To my dismay, it was a woman. Clear as day, I remember running alongside the Thruway as a large number of Syracuse fans chased me from behind. I must have run all the way back to Fort Slocum. Such was the volatility of the ethnic fans during that period.

Chapter 5
High Above Cayuga's Waters
1957-1960

I was discharged from the U.S. Army in August of 1957. My brother Howie had been selected to try out for the U.S. National Soccer Team in 1955 while I was going through basic training with the 101st Airborne at Fort Jackson, SC.

Figure 23
Howie Article about Tryouts with
US National Team
Buffalo Evening News

He later became a Soccer All-American at Penn State. I had wanted to go to Penn State all my life. Howie contacted his coach, Ken Hosterman, who had replaced the legendary Coach Bill Jefferies. He asked Coach Hosterman if a scholarship could be available for me. I did not hear back from Howie or Coach Hosterman until it was too late.

U.S. Soccer Coach
BILL JEFFREY

Figure 24
The Legendary Penn St
Coach Bill Jefferies
Penn State Soccer History

Herb Mols, my Park School High School Athletic Director, was aware of my dilemma and suggested I consider Cornell. He graduated from Cornell in 1937. Later, in 1975, he co-founded the New York Empire Games. He was a coach for the U.S. National Basketball Team in 1971(Pan American Games) and a coach on the U.S. National Basketball Team (1972). I told Coach Mols I was interested but did not believe I could be accepted by Cornell at such a late date. I told him I would apply. At the time, I had no idea of Coach Mol's persuasive powers.

Figure 25
Coach Herb Mols
1975 NY State Empire Games
Park School of Buffalo History

What a surprise! Shortly after submitting my application, I received word from Cornell that I had been accepted as a student at its School of Agriculture. It also granted me a Leadership Scholarship. The New York State University (SUNY) system had five of its colleges on campus at the time and those colleges were very popular because they had very low tuition rates compared to the private colleges at the university. The tuition for the Agriculture College was $450 per semester. I quickly accepted Cornell's offer and shortly thereafter I received a call from Howie saying that Penn State would like to offer me a full soccer scholarship. It was too late to accept the offer since I had committed to Cornell.

Now that I was accepted by Cornell, I had to find a place to live and a job to provide for my food and other expenses. Luckily, Tom Webb, a soccer teammate from Buffalo and longtime friend, came up with a solution. While I was in the service, he had been accepted by Cornell and was a member of the Delta Upsilon Fraternity (DU). He convinced the fraternity to provide me with a job as a dishwasher for my meals. It would also allow me to sleep on the outside porch. I agreed to its terms, even though sleeping outside through most of my first semester involved temperatures often below freezing. Space in the DU house opened up in early 1958 after I had pledged the fraternity. I was then allowed to move into the DU house.

I remember going to soccer practice the first day. Cornell had an eclectic soccer team, with players from Jamaica, Rome, the Virgin Islands, Cuba, El Salvador, Liberia and the Philippines. It had two All-Americans on the team, Al Strata from Rome, Italy and Clyde Beckford from Jamaica. Al was the captain of our team in 1958. Since graduating from Cornell, he has had a marvelous business career as a hotel executive, first as President of the Princess Hotels and since 1985 as the President and Chief Executive Officer of the Beverly Hills Hotel.

Figure 26
Cornell Soccer Team – 1958
Ron 2nd row second from Left

Clive Beckford was a terrific player and we became close during my first year on the team. Often, we would meet for lunch and I usually would treat him. Clive, unfortunately, died between his junior and senior year of congenital heart failure. The school established the Clive Beckford Memorial Award, presented each year to the soccer team's outstanding soccer player. I was its first recipient in 1959.

Figure 27
Clive Beckford Memorial Award Presented by
Bob Kane, Athletic Director and future President
Of the U.S. Olympic Committee and Coach George Patte
Cornell Daily Sun Newspaper

Each year since graduation, I received a warm Christmas card from his family in Jamaica. In 1978, I attended a business meeting in Puerto Rico and decided to fly into Jamaica on my way home. The Beckford's address was Ocho Rios, Jamaica. The Playboy hotel was the only hotel in Ocho Rios at the time so I made a reservation there.

I settled into my hotel room and the next morning I asked the front desk if they could direct me to the Beckford's residence. The clerk smiled politely at me and told me the family owned all the beachfront between the hotel and Ocho Rios, and I would have to be more specific about where I wanted to go. Wow! He gave me their telephone number and Clive's mother answered the phone. She went wild when she heard my name and said she would send a car right over to pick me up.

Shortly after the telephone call, a black Rolls Royce pulled into the arrival door. The driver got out and asked if I was Ron Maierhofer. I responded, yes and he drove me to the Beckford residence, about two miles away. I was shocked! It was a huge plantation with a huge house. There were a large number of family members and staff in the driveway as we drove up. I was welcomed with open arms by all and they escorted me into their home and gave me a tour. I was shocked again! Each of the rooms they showed, including bathrooms, had a picture of Clive and myself.

As it turned out, the Beckford family was one of the wealthiest families in Jamaica. They controlled the import of all automotive after-market products like tires, oil, batteries, and spark plugs. The plantation was famous since the filming of the James Bond spy thriller, "Live or Let Die" with Sean Connery. I had a wonderful breakfast with the family. Clive was always a gentleman and modest. He never mentioned his family and I never asked. I assumed he was an economically disadvantaged student at Cornell. The moral is never assume!

It was quite an experience attending Cornell. I worked several jobs to put myself through school and received no assistance from my parents. Those jobs included dishwasher, salad maker, house steward, library monitor, and operating a business that offered after-study snacks and sandwiches to several fraternity houses. There was still time to play varsity soccer and lacrosse, study, and have a few nights out doing what I love best, dancing. I graduated from Cornell with no debt, which is impossible today for most families with multiple siblings. My starting salary in 1960 as a graduate of the Industrial and Labor Relations (ILR) College was $510 per month, the highest starting salary in my ILR graduating class.

Early in the spring of 1959, I was selected to compete in the United States Soccer Federation's eastern tryouts in Brooklyn. Those selected would earn a spot on the U.S. 1959 Eastern All-Star Soccer Team and compete for the U.S. National Soccer Team. The eastern team would compete in St. Louis against all-star players from regions representing the mid-west, the far-west, and the south. Finalists would be selected and would become the 1959 U.S. National Soccer Team.

The USSF eastern tryouts had all-star players from eastern-based amateur clubs and leagues, the armed forces, and eastern colleges. I was selected for the Eastern All-Star Soccer Team, which then competed in St. Louis against the

Western All-Star Soccer Team, the Midwest All-Star Soccer Team and the Southern All-Star Soccer Team. The final eighteen players would be selected for the U.S. National Soccer Team and, subject to major injury, represent the United States in the 1959 Pan American Games to be held in Chicago and the 1960 Olympic Elimination Games to be held before the games started in Rome. I made the final squad and became a member of the 1959 U.S. National Soccer Team.

Good Prospects For 1960

Cornell Olympians

By ROBERT J. KANE

Director of Athletics, Cornell University
Manager, 1952 U.S. Olympic Track Team

Cornell has been uncommonly well represented on the past two Olympic squads and there appears to be a good chance it will be again for the Games in Rome, Italy, August 25–September 11, 1960.

Four Cornellians participated in the Pan-American Games held in Chicago August 27–September 7 and three of them won championships. They were Albert W. Hall '56, hammer throw; Irvin Roberson '58, broad jump, and David C. Auble '60, 125.5 pounds in wrestling. Ronald P. Maierhofer '60 was a member of the soccer squad which won four of six games and placed third behind Argentina and Brazil.

Hall set a new Pan-American Games record in the hammer by throwing 195 feet 11 inches and was tied by Harold Connolly, 1956 Olympic champion. Hall's second best throw of 192-4½ was better than Connolly's next best of 191-5 so he was awarded the Pan-American title. Roberson's magnificent leap of 26 feet 2 inches defeated Gregory Bell of USA, 1956 Olympic champion, and he became one of a select baker's dozen who have ever achieved the rarified 26 feet distance. And this likewise set a new Pan-American standard. Auble was one of very few undergraduate winners of a Pan-American championship and thus added this international distinction to an already distinguished collegiate record which includes two Eastern Intercollegiate Wrestling Association titles and one National Collegiate championship.

The only one of this talented quartet who has already won his place on the 1960 Olympic team is Maierhofer. The U.S.A. team in 1960 Games will remain the same as that selected for the Pan-American Games, barring serious injury or some other incapacitating reason. It will be necessary for the U.S.A. entry to win a North American zone qualifying round before going to Rome. This is one of the many new features of stiffer qualification for the 1960 Games designed to cut down the huge entry list. The winner of a two-game series with Mexico goes to Rome for the quarter finals.

Dave Auble · · · · · Ron Maierhofer

Figure 28
Bob Kane Article 1960
Cornell Daily Sun

Figure 29
U.S. National Soccer Team 1959
3rd Pan American Games – Chicago
1960 United States Olympic Book

The 1959 Pan American Games were held in Chicago. Our U.S. National Soccer Team won four of the six matches it played, winning the first international medal in soccer for the United States since the 1930 FIFA World Cup competition. During the competition, we defeated Brazil 5-3 on August 31 and Mexico 4-2. Our team won a bronze medal. Al Zerhusen, who I later played against in the Greater Los Angeles Soccer League, scored ten goals for us. Also on the team was Janos "Red" Snylek" with whom I played against when he played for the Rochester Ukrainians. Also, Rolf Ganger who played with me on the Coast Rangers in the Greater Los Angeles Soccer League. I was injured in the first game but still managed to play in five of the six matches.

There would be notable future coaches at Cornell in the later years after I graduated. Dan Wood would coach Cornell Soccer from 1971 to 1975 and would later become famous for adding Bruce Arena, twice U.S. National Soccer Team coach, to the 1974 Cornell Soccer team. Dan also coached the Colorado Caribous and Atlanta Chiefs in the NASL.

Figure 30
Dan Wood, Coach of Cornell and the
NASL Colorado Caribou
Dan is 2ND in on top right
Colorado Caribou Marketing Department

Bruce Arena played for Dan for several years. Bruce was inducted into the Cornell Athletic Hall of Fame in 1986.

Figure 31
Bruce Arena's Induction Class of 1986
Cornell Athletic Hall of Fame
Men's Lacrosse and Men's Soccer
Cornell Athletic Department

Cornell summed up Bruce at the induction ceremony, "Bruce was All-Ivy first team as a lacrosse midfielder and soccer goaltender in his senior year. A tri-captain and team MVP in 1972, he was also All-Ivy first team in lacrosse as a junior. In 1972 he was the team's fifth-leading scorer and finished third in his final year. He was named to the All-America second team as a senior and received honorable mention honors the previous season. In soccer, he was named the team's most valuable player in 1972 when the Big Red reached the semifinals of the NCAA championships. He was named the tourney's outstanding defensive player.

Drafted by the New York Cosmos in 1973, Bruce played for Seattle and Tacoma in the pro leagues. He toured Italy and Israel with the U.S. National team in 1972... In May of 1978, he was appointed head soccer and assistant lacrosse coach at the University of Virginia. A graduate of Carey High School and Nassau Community College, he resided in Franklin Square, N.Y. as an undergraduate."

I was also inducted into the Cornell Hall of Fame in 1986.

Figure 32
Ronald Maierhofer
Induction Class of 1986
Cornell Athletic Hall of Fame
Men's Soccer
Cornell Athletic Department

Cornell's comments about me at the induction ceremony were "An outstanding soccer forward, he was chosen to the All-America second team in 1959. A two-time All-Ivy first team pick, he was an All-New York State selection his senior year. Captain and the team's MVP in 1959, he led the squad in scoring that year and was runner-up as a junior. He was a midfielder on the varsity lacrosse team in 1958 and 1959. He was a member of the U.S. soccer squad which placed third in the 1959 Pan American Games, and won a place on the 1960 Olympic team. He played pro soccer with Toronto of the Canadian Soccer Association. He is a graduate of the Park School and resided in Buffalo, N.Y., while attending Cornell."

My four sons were at the induction ceremony into the Cornell Athletic Hall of Fame in Ithaca on September 19, 1996.

Figure 33
Cornell Athletic Hall of Fame
Ceremony September 19, 1986
Sons Jeff, Tim, Ron, Scott, Craig

Bruce's sidekick, while he was the U.S. National Team Coach, was Dave Sarachan. Dave coached Cornell Soccer from 1989 to 1997. The United States Soccer Federation, on October 24, 2017, named Dave Sarachan as the interim U.S. National Soccer Team Coach. Dave worked under Bruce Arena during two stints with the U.S. Soccer Team, as well as stops at the University of Virginia, D.C. United, and the LA Galaxy. Sarachan also was the head coach at Cornell University from 1988 until 1997. At the professional level, he served as manager of the Chicago Fire from late 2002 through 2007.

Figure 34
Dave Sarachan
U.S. National Soccer Team Coach 2017
USSF

Dave invited me to play in Cornell's Soccer Alumni Game in 1997. It was to be his last season at Cornell. I played in the game and at the age of sixty-two, Dave complimented me and said I held my own against the young varsity players. The Team had a reunion party later and Dave asked me to present the Clive Beckford Memorial Player to that year's recipient as Cornell's outstanding soccer player.

I was fortunate to receive several soccer awards while at Cornell and after graduation. The Ivy League, Intercollegiate East, and New York State named me to their All Intercollegiate Soccer Teams in 1959.

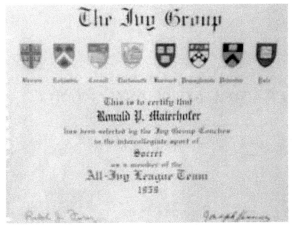

Figure 35
1959 All-Ivy Team

Figure 36
The National Soccer Coaches of America
All-American Soccer Team 1959

WALK OF FAME
CERTIFICATE OF AUTHENTICITY

THIS CERTIFICATE ACKNOWLEDGES THAT
A BRICK HAS BEEN RESERVED IN THE WALK OF FAME AS:

Ronald Maierhofer
US Natl Team 59-60
All-Amer. Cornell

THIS CONTRIBUTION HAS BEEN
RECOGNIZED AND APPRECIATED BY:

Figure 37
U.S. National Soccer Hall of Fame
Hall of Fame Brick

While a student, the university selected me as a student representative to its Board of Directors. The Executive Board of Cornell Student Government also invited me to a private reception for former President Harry S. Truman. These private receptions were affectionately known as fireside chats.

Mr. Ronald Maierhofer

The Executive Board of Cornell Student Government

cordially invites you to attend a

Private Reception for

PRESIDENT HARRY S. TRUMAN

on Monday, April 18, 1960

from 9:30 to 11:00 p. m.

in the

Memorial Room of Willard Straight Hall

Invitations will be required for admittance

Figure 38
Harry S. Truman Fireside Chat
Cornell, April 18, 1960

On June 14, 1960, my class elected me as President of the 1960 Alumni Association. I served for five years after graduation.

FRIDAY, JUNE 10, 1960

1960 Men's Alumni Officers Elected for Five-Year Terms

OFFICERS OF THE 1960 MEN'S ALUMNI CLASS COUNCIL are shown above. Seated are Ronald Maierhofer (left), class president James McGuire, reunion chairman. Peter Snyder, class correspondent (left), Gerald Cerand, class secretary and Charles Parsons, class vice president, stand behind.

Figure 39
Elected President of Alumni Club 1960

I was also named to Cornell's Athletic Advisory Board in 1997 for a three-year term. All of these awards mostly due to my successes at playing my sport. A first-generation blue-collar German-American's dream, achieved by working hard, perseverance, and luck!

Figure 40
U.S. National Soccer Team 1959
1960 United States Olympic Book

Figure 41
George Brown U.S.
National Soccer Team 1959
Secretary and Member
U.S. National Soccer Hall of Fame

Figure 42
Ron with Miss USA
1959 Pan-Am Games

Figure 43
Ron and Alex Ely
1959 U.S. National Soccer Team
U.S. National Soccer Hall of Fame

The 1959 U.S. National Team Relaxing after Practice

Figure 44
1959 U.S. National Soccer Team
Relaxing after Practice

Chapter 6
Buffalo Beef on Weck
1961 - 1963

My graduation from Cornell was in the spring of 1960. I had been offered an opportunity with the Standard Oil Company of Ohio (SOHIO) as a management trainee in Cleveland, Ohio. Several months later, I was transferred to its Cincinnati regional office to continue my training.

I played a few months with the Cincinnati Kolping Soccer Club while employed by SOHIO. Later, after making the U.S. National Soccer Team, I found out that Al Zerhusen had played for a short time with the Kolping Club in the 1950's. Al had played in Germany as a child and settled in Cincinnati with his parents in 1950. Like me, he was drafted into the Army in late 1950. He was transferred back to Cincinnati while playing for the Armed Forces Team and was selected in 1954 for the U.S. National Soccer Team. He later played for the Cincinnati Kolping Soccer Club. Al was again selected for the U.S. team in 1956 and competed in the 1956 Summer Olympics. When the games ended he moved to Los Angeles.

By late 1960, I had decided the career direction with Standard Oil was not for me and relocated back to Buffalo, N.Y. My brother, Howie, went through a similar transition with the Armstrong Cork Company, located in Lancaster, PA. He also relocated back to Buffalo.

While in Buffalo, we expanded our father's meat business into the frozen dinner market. Buffalo is known for two major food items, Buffalo wings and beef-on-weck. Buffalo wings were initially invented in 1961 by a local restaurant called the Anchor Bar. The company never trademarked its invention and now Buffalo wings are a worldwide food commodity.

The other food item famous in Buffalo is called Beef-on-Weck. It is sliced roast beef added to a German hard roll called a Kummelweck. The Kummelweck roll is a hard roll and is topped with coarse salt and caraway seeds. Howie and I discovered how to quick freeze the sliced roast beef with its gravy. We packaged the frozen product and sold it to most of the chain stores in Western N.Y. The two major competitors at the time were Banquet and Swanson TV dinners. Their products focused on chicken and turkey dinners.

I continued to play with the Simon Pure team, which was the successor to the Buffalo Becks. By then I was married and my first son Scott was born in Buffalo. Carborundum, a national abrasive company headquartered in a Buffalo suburb, recruited me to enter its sales management training program. It trained me for six months and transferred me to Cincinnati where my wife's family lived. The Kolping Soccer Club was located on Winton Rd, close to our home, and I played for the club until I relocated to Los Angeles in 1963.

Figure 45
Kolping Soccer Team Logo
Kolping Website

Chapter 7
California, Here We Come
1963-1971

1963-67

By 1963, my career had taken me to California. We relocated from Cincinnati to Los Angeles and found temporary housing in La Mirada, a suburb. Shortly after, we located to permanent housing in Whittier, California. We had arrived with two sons, Scott and Jeff, in tow. Tim and Craig were later born while we lived in California. Sons Scott and Jeff were born in 1961 and 1962 and were not yet ready to get involved with soccer. By 1966 they were involved in recreational t-ball. There were no local youth soccer leagues in our neighborhood at that time for preschoolers or kindergarteners.

We developed a friendship with a couple, Vic and Geline DiVirgilio, who lived a few doors away. Vic was quite the character and worked for a wholesale wine distributor. His territory was Hollywood and he called on roughly forty restaurants on the Hollywood strip close to the famous Hollywood and Vine intersection. I would often meet him for lunch in Hollywood.

Vic and I were having lunch one day in Hollywood when a friend of his approached our table. Vic introduced us and proceeded to inform his friend of my soccer background. His friend said he managed a soccer team called the Maccabi's and would I be interested in playing for it. I told him I was not Jewish but he said that didn't matter. They had one or two other players who weren't Jewish. He mentioned that the team trained on Wednesday's at a field close to the new Dodger Stadium (built in 1962) called Chavez Ravine. I told him I would be there Wednesday.

The following Wednesday, I showed up at the field for the tryout practice and was pleasantly surprised. The team had an excellent group of players and had been formed during the early 60s by European immigrant players. It was an average team at that time but later, in the early 70s and early 80s, became the only soccer club to win five National Challenge Cup (U.S. Open) Championships.

Figure 46
The Maccabi's in the Early 70's
Web Photo

The manager asked me to join the team. He said it was a semi-professional team, playing in the Greater Los Angeles Soccer League (GLASL). They could not afford to pay much money but suggested another alternative. He would pay me for playing by giving me seven cases of liquor if I signed, and a bottle of Chivas Regal for every goal I scored. I had an excellent job as a Western Divisional Sales Manager of an abrasive company and didn't need the extra cash. I quickly accepted his offer!

I remember meeting an interesting team player at that tryout. His name was Hans Gudegast; he was a German immigrant who arrived in the U.S. in 1959. He considered himself the token non-Jewish player on the team. Now the team had two! Hans was a wonderful player and said he also won the German National Track and Field Championship. I shrugged that off since many players coming from Europe purported to have been top athletes and usually said they played for first division clubs in their country.

Hans said at the time that he was an actor and was playing a role in a TV series since 1965 called The Rat Patrol. I thought at the time he was joking. I was surprised to find out he portrayed Hans Dietrich, the German officer on that TV series. A few years later, after I had left the team, he changed his name and used a stage name, Eric Braeden. Many wives or girlfriends know him as Victor on the longest lasting TV series, *The Young and the Restless*. His first movie under his new name was *100 Rifles*, starring Rachael Welch, Burt Reynolds, Jim Brown, and Fernando Lamas. Since then he has become an international legend in the movie industry. He still is a soccer nut after all these years.

Figure 47
Hans Gudegast – Eric Braeden
Web Article

I played for another team during this time period in California. It was called the Coast Rangers and it played in the Pacific Soccer League and later the GLASL. It won the league championship in 1966. I do not remember much about that time frame with that team except that one of its players was named Rolf Ganger. Rolf was a teammate of mine on the 1959 U.S. National Soccer Team which played in the 1959 Pan American Games and he also played on the 1960 Olympic preliminary round against Mexico. Rolf had also been a teammate of Al Zerhusan on the Los Angeles Kickers.

Zerhusan was the leading scorer of the GLASL for thirteen years, playing with the LA Scots and the LA Kickers. He was born in Brooklyn but at the age of 5 years moved to Germany with his parents. He returned to the United States in 1950 and played for the Armed Forces Team and the Cincinnati Kolping Soccer Club. I played for the Kolping club in 1960 while living in Cincinnati.

Al was on the U.S. National Team in 1956 (Olympic Team), the U.S. National Team (World Cup Team) in 1957, 1959 (Pan American Team), 1962 U.S. World Cup Team and was inducted into the National Soccer Hall of Fame in 1978. He scored ten goals for us when the U.S. played in the 1959 Pan American Games. Al is now eighty-six years old but still involved in soccer as a Director of the Los Angeles Soccer Club, the successor of the LA Kickers.

The United States Men's National Soccer Team, often referred to as the USMNT, represents the United States in international soccer. It is controlled by the United States Soccer Federation and competes in CONCACAF (the Confederation of North, Central American and Caribbean Association Football). The U.S. team has appeared in ten FIFA World Cups (Courtesy of Wikipedia.)

Figure 48
Al Zerhusan LA Kickers – 1960's
U.S. National Soccer Hall of Fame
LA Times Newspaper 1960's

1968-1971

At the end of 1967, I was promoted to Vice President of Sales by my company and transferred back to the company's headquarters in Dayton, Ohio. We found a nice home in Centerville, a southern suburb. There was limited soccer in the area at the time and our sons Scott and Jeff were now old enough to play soccer. I helped found the Centerville Soccer Club, which merged into the Centerville Recreation Soccer Club in 1971. I was able to play the 1969 and 1970 seasons with a men's team called the Dayton Aviators. It played in the Southern Ohio Adult Soccer Association and it was the only team on which I played that was made up of all U.S. born players. Most teams were still ethnically based in those years.

My most memorable moment was playing against an Italian team one Sunday afternoon. My wife and four sons were seated on a blanket, watching the game. An Italian player was fouled by one of our players close to me. The player on the Italian team took the back of his hand and gave a karate shot to the throat of our player who fouled him. Since I was the closest to the contact between them, I rushed in to defend our player and gave the Italian a kick where it hurt the most. Suddenly, several of the Italian team players were chasing me and I remember jumping over the blanket on which my family was sitting. Nothing had changed in amateur soccer. It was World War II all over again!

Chapter 8
These Dallas Boots Are…!
1971-1975

My years in Dallas were to be the most important for my transition from a player to a player-coach and later to a sports team owner. They were equally important in shaping my views towards developing youth soccer club and soccer club ownership.

The previous year, while living in Centerville, Ohio, I received a phone call from Pete Judd, an old friend and business acquaintance. Pete had become the Regional Sales Manager of Information Handling Services in Los Angeles, which was the information technology company for a holding company called Indianhead. He indicated that he had a sales management opening in Dallas and asked if I was interested. My family and I talked it through and decided that it would be a great opportunity. We moved to Dallas in early 1971 and located a nice home for rent while we looked for permanent housing. It was located in Richardson, a Dallas suburb. This was the beginning of my long time efforts to build youth soccer in the U.S.A.

My sons had expanded their soccer careers in Dayton, Ohio. When we moved to Dallas, the boys wanted to know where they could play on a team. At that time in Dallas' youth soccer history, there were no competitive/travel leagues in Northern Texas. There were several local recreational leagues and The Richardson Soccer Association had a recreational team, the Prairie Creek Rangers, which was close to the kid's elementary school. I quickly arranged for the kids to play on it and I was also recruited by its coach, Jack Schletzer, to help out and take over coaching the team.

Dallas had a professional team at that time called the Dallas Tornado.

They played in the North American Soccer League (NASL) and won its championship in 1971, and they won the NASL championship again in 1973. Little did I know at the time that many of those team members would be involved in my later soccer playing and team ownership life? Its coach at the time was Ron Newman. The goalkeeper was Ken Cooper, Jr. and field players included Kyle Rote, Jr., Roy Turner, John Best, Mike Renshaw and Jim Benedek. Joe Echelle was its General Manager and Neil Cohen was the team's trainer.

Ron Newman was later to become involved with me in developing the Richardson Sparta Soccer Club. After a short stint with me at the Sparta Club, Ron moved on and became the winningest soccer coach for the NASL's San Diego Sockers. He won sixteen indoor soccer champions and later was inducted into the Soccer Hall of Fame. The San Diego Sockers joined the Major League Indoor Soccer League (MISL) IN 1988. Ron is now eighty-two years old.

Ken Cooper, Sr. was the goalkeeper on the team. He was on the 1973 U.S. National Team. Ken later became the coach of the MISL's Baltimore Blast during my Avalanche years and continued as its coach to the early 1990's. His son, Ken Cooper, Jr. played in the Major Soccer League (MLS). Ken now owns a wine importing business with fellow teammate Mike Renshaw. Mike was also on the Dallas Tornado and another U.S. National Team player in 1973.

Roy Turner, born in England in 1941, was a field player on the Dallas Tornado and also was on the U.S. National Team in 1973. Roy was to become another MISL member and coached the Wichita Wings from 1969-1978. They had a great indoor team and the Denver Avalanche played them several times.

John Best, born in Liverpool, England, played on those Dallas Tornado teams and was on the U.S. National Team in 1973. Later, John played for the MISL Seattle Sounders during 1974-76 and then became the General Manager of the MISL Vancouver Whitecaps. He founded the Tacoma Indoor Soccer Club in 1983, called the Tacoma Stars. The Tacoma Stars acquired the Denver Avalanche from us in 1983. John died in 2014.

Jim (Janos) Benedek was born in Hungary and became a U.S. citizen. He attended Ithaca College. Cornell, which I attended, was also in Ithaca NY. Jim was on the U.S. National Teams in 1968 and 1969. He played for the Dallas Tornado 1970-1973. Later that year, while playing for an amateur team, the Dallas Rangers, we played a friendly scrimmage game against Dallas Tornado at the Dallas Cowboy's Stadium in Irving, Texas. Jim was guarding me and talking the talk – calling me an old man! I was forty years old at the time. I had the best goal of my career at the time, a half volley shot from about forty yards from the goal. He did not talk the talk after that goal, but later joined my Richardson Sparta Soccer Club as a coach. That Dallas Ranger team won state amateur men's championships from 1971-1974. I switched teams in 1975 and joined the Richardson United who played in the North Texas Premier League.

Joe Echelle immigrated to the United States from Austria in the late 1940's. He was a serious student of the game although he never played. He became the General Manager of the Dallas Tornado during its glory years 1969-1974. He later became the General Manager of the MISL Denver Dynamos. When it folded, he became the GM of the NASL'S Caribous of Colorado. He started the Notre Dame University Soccer Club and became its leader for almost forty years. My grandson, Kyle Maierhofer, attended Notre Dame during Joe's dynasty.

Figure 49
Joe Echelle GM
NASL Dallas Tornado 1969-1974
Notre Dame Athletic Department

Finally, the Dallas Tornado team trainer was Neil Cohen. He later played for the Dallas Tornado in 1974 and played in the NASL for 8 seasons. He was the youngest American player to be signed by the NASL. My team, the Denver Avalanche of the MISL, signed him in 1981. He played two seasons for the Avalanche.

Figure 50
Neil Cohen Denver Avalanche

NASL 1971 Champion Dallas Tornado

Back Row (L to R): Lamar Hant, V-P; Phil Tinney, Ray Bloomfield, Frank Huson, Bobby Moffat, Tibor Molnar, Gabbo Gavric, Mike Renshaw, Joe Echelle, Gen. Mgr. Front Row (L to R): Ken Cooper, Jim Benedek, Oreca, John Best, Ron Newman, Coach; Dick Hall, Roy Turner, Luiz Juracy, Tony McLoughlin.

Figure 51
Dallas Tornado
NASL Champions 1971
Dallas News

Center Front: Neil Cohen, Trainer. First Row (left to right): Ken Cooper, Jim Benedek, John Best, Roy Turner, Bob Ridley, Luiz Juracy, Ilija Mitic, Mike Renshaw. Second Row (left to right): Dr. John Graham, Mohammad Attaih, Kyle Rote Jr., Julio Alas, Bobby Moffat, Otey Cannon, Ray Bloomfield, Edwardo Constantino, Fredrico Garcia, Ron Newman, Coach.

Figure 52
Dallas Tornado
NASL Champions 1973
Dallas News

Kyle Rote Jr. was also on the Dallas Tornado team in 1973. Kyle's dad, Kyle Rote Sr., presented me with an award while I was at Cornell. Kyle Sr. played for the NY Giants as a wide receiver and after his playing career was a co-announcer on TV with Curt Gowdy during the first two super bowls.

Figure 53
Kyle Rote, Sr.
New York Giants – NFL

Tornado 1974 Kyle Rote Jr.

Figure 45
Kyle Rote, Jr.
NASL Dallas Tornado 1974
Avalanche Announcer 1982
Dallas News

Kyle grew up in Dallas and played on the Black Bandits youth team. He went on to college playing at the University of the South in Swanee, TN. He returned to Dallas and played in scrimmages against the Dallas Tornado. He played in a scrimmage with the Dallas Rangers, a team I was playing for at the time. We played the game in the Dallas Cowboys Football Stadium in Arlington, TX.

Kyle signed with the Dallas Tornado in 1973 and was the league's Rookie of the Year. He played in the NASL until 1977, when he retired. I remember him in the Super Star competition on ABC. By that time, he was generally considered America's first soccer superstar. He participated in three Super Star Competitions during the 1970s and won all of them. He competed against O.J. Simpson (NFL), Pete Rose (Baseball), Lynn Swann (NFL), Roger Staubach (NFL), Jim Palmer (Baseball), John Havlecek (NBA) and Stan Smith (Tennis). Kyle won $185,000 from those competitions. Comparatively, the average NASL player at the time was making $8,000 per season. Kyle retired in 1977 at the age of 26. He became our TV color announcer for the Denver Avalanche in 1982. Kyle later became a sports agent and is still working at it today.

Richardson Soccer Association 1971-1975

We relocated to Dallas, Texas in early 1971 and found a home in the Prairie Creek suburb. My sons, Scott and Jeff, quickly signed up and played on the Prairie Creek Rangers in the Richardson Soccer Association's (RSA) recreational league. Its coach at the time, Jack Schletzer, recruited me to coach the team shortly after we arrived and I coached the team from 1971–to June 1975. He also recruited me to help him Coach JJ Pearce H.S in 1973.

Staff photos by Chad Fergus
OTHER AWARD WINNERS at the Seventh Annual Spring Sports Banquet honor Pearce athletes were in top photo (from left): Assistant soccer coach Jack Johanns Most Valuable Player David Musgrove, Perseverance winner Jon Harris, and Assist coach Ron Maierhofer. The top volleyball player was Sherri Blanchard pictured bottom photo at left. The girls track award winners (also bottom photo) were M Outstanding Sandra Lyman (center) and Perseverance Katherine Kelly. The banq was sponsored by the J.J. Pearce Booster Club Saturday night in the Mustang Com

Figure 55
Assistant Coach JJ Pearce H.S.
Sports Banquet 1971
Photo by Pearce H.S. Alumni

North Texas had many youth recreational soccer teams at that time. Our Prairie Creek Rangers dominated the Richardson Soccer Association teams in those years and won championships from 1971-1974. The team was primarily made up of Prairie Creek Elementary School players who played together for many years. My sons, Scott, Jeff, and Tim, have maintained close relationships with those team members since that time. Team players included Scott Elgin, Robbie Harper, Nick Solomos, Mark Johannsen, Dean Madden, Danny Meeker, Toby Grove, Rick Toynbee, Mike Semmer, Brad Scott, Brad Long, David Franze, John Blankenship, Joe Renfro, Drew Pittman, Glenn Morrow, Mike Heath, John Hagen, Barry Gillam, Shaw Sudden, and Bill Pierce.

Figure 56
JJ Pearce H.S.
Assistant Coach 1973-74

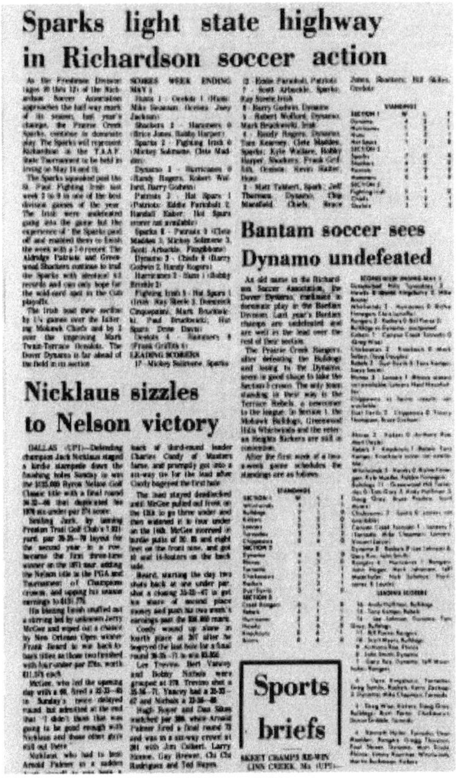

Sparks light state highway in Richardson soccer action

Bantam soccer sees Dynamo undefeated

Nicklaus sizzles to Nelson victory

Sports briefs

Figure 57
Richardson Soccer League
Richardson Daily News
March 9, 1971

The North Texas Soccer Association, in early 1975, received an invitation to the National Junior Soccer Championships for U14 boys All-Star Select Teams. The competition was being held in Denver, Colorado, with teams invited from Los Angeles, Memphis, Chicago, Jacksonville, FL, Miami and San Antonio. The team was to be coached by Jan Block. Scott Maierhofer, Jeff Maierhofer, and Robbie Harper were selected for the team. The team was to travel with the NASL Dallas Tornado to Colorado. The North Texas U14 Select Team went 8-0 and also defeated two Denver U16 select teams scheduled to tour Europe.

head squad

Jan Blok, coach of the boys under 14 North Texas All Star soccer team, has released the names of the 32 boys which will represent North Texas this summer against Los Angeles, Memphis, Chicago, Jacksonville, Miami and San Antonio. There are approximately 3000 boys of this age group playing soccer in North exas.

Local Richardson boys who have been selected include Robie Harper, Scott and Jeff Maierhofer, Tom Jones, Tom Durst, Nick Solomos, Brad Scott, Greg Sumblin, Mark Meeker, Mike Chapman, Bill Pierce, Mike Semmer, Calvin Trim, Brian Ervine, Toby Grove and Barry Gillam.

The team entered its first competition at Denver and played eight games without a defeat. Two of the wins were against Denver under 16 select teams that are going to Europe in September.

Figure 58
North Texas All-Star Selections – 1975
Richardson Daily News

The personal closeness among the players on the Prairie Creek Rangers has lasted a lifetime. Robbie Harper, one of the most popular players and friend of many of his teammates, died in 2014. The Richardson *Daily News* wrote an article on May 1st at the time and displayed a photograph. Wrote the News:

J.J. Pearce High School alumni, who graduated in the mid-to-late-1970s, gathered on the school's soccer field on May 1. The group includes (back row) Luis Sifuentes, Wade Saulsberry, Bradley Anderson, Toby Grove, David Musgrove, Tom Gray, (front row) Kelley Meeker, Tommy Jones, Brad Scott, Mike Anderson, Craig Rind and Mike Tannery. After their friend and fellow teammate, Rob Harper, died in January 2014 members of the group began efforts to establish an award and memorial fund in his honor.

Figure 59
Rob Harper Memorial - Pearce H.S.
Richardson Daily News
May 14, 2014

By mid-1975, I felt that the North Texas recreational leagues were not providing an environment for improving players. Almost all of the teams were being coached by parents of players. I decided that I would try to solve that problem. I came up with the idea of a new travel club and named it the Richardson Sparta Soccer Club. I knew that every North Texas recreational team had at least one or two players who had the potential to significantly improve. Usually, those kids had fathers who were the coaches of those teams. I called Ron Newman and shared my idea. I wanted to have a club with outstanding professional coaches and wanted to attract the better players. Ron agreed to help out.

I called a number of recreational coaches and invited them to a meeting at Prairie Creek Elementary School. Thirty or more of the recreational coaches showed up, as did Ron Newman. I explained the concept to them and they bought into the idea. We then organized the new club with articles and bylaws at a later meeting. At the organizational meeting on July 4, 1975, we elected the officers. I convinced a number of non-soccer oriented friends to consider running for the Executive Board. During the organizational meeting, the attendees voted on the Executive Board. Elected were Gus Stearns, President, Frank Gangi, V.P. Public Relations, John Kemendo, Treasurer, John Miller, V.P. Facilities and Equipment, Ed Coale, V.P Player Selection and Mildred White, Secretary. I was elected the Vice President of Coaching and Training.

Figure 60
Start of Richardson Sparta Soccer Club
July 27, 1995
Richardson Daily News

We decided to have our first tryouts in August 1975. Ron Newman agreed to coach in the new club, as did several other professional coaches including:

1. Jan Block – Holland National R.A.F. Team
2. Mike Kinch – Former Oxford University Coach
3. Jimmie Benedek – U.S. World Cup, Olympic and Pan Am Teams – Coach Southern Methodist University

4. Dick Hall – Dallas Tornado and Greenhill School Coach
5. Bene – 1st Division Professional Player
6. John Antoinisse – Coach - J.J. Pearce H.S. -Player TX Premier League Adult Champions, Dallas Rangers
7. Luigi Mungioli – Columbia 1st Division Player – Dallas Premier League Champions, Dallas Rangers
8. Richard Mungioli – Coach, J.J. Pearce H.S.
9. Joe Ognjanac – U.S. National Team – NASL player
10. Jim Waiters - NIA, Division II National Champion

Figure 61
Sparta Selection of Coaches
July 1975
Richardson Daily News

We held our first tryouts on August 2, 1975 for boys and girls. Three hundred players showed up for the tryouts and we selected players for ten boys and girls teams ages U12-U19. Teams were formed and we were short two coaches for the Sparta Girls U16 and U14 Girls Teams. I was asked to coach the teams and agreed. Prior to this period, I had never coached girl's teams and trained them as I would a boy team. We did not have National Championships in those days but did have Regional Championships. Both girl teams went on to win Regional Championships and I believe several of the players later played for the University of North Carolina and participated in its early successes.

The U16 Sparta Boys Team, with Scott and Jeff Maierhofer on it, won the North Texas Championships in October 1975. Scott was 14 years old at the time. A few weeks later, the Sparta Club sponsored the 1st Inter-City Invitational Tournament, played on Thanksgiving weekend. We arranged to get Finn Air Airlines to sponsor the tournament. Teams played from Aurora, Colorado, Denver, Colorado, St. Louis, Tulsa, Oklahoma City and outstanding North Texas squads. Several months later, I was promoted by my company. I worked in Denver and came home on the weekends. The family moved to Denver in early 1976.

The Colorado School of Mines hosted a USSF coaching school in 1976, which I attended and received a National B License. I also received a lifetime National C license. I later became the Director of Coaching for the Colorado State Youth Soccer Association.

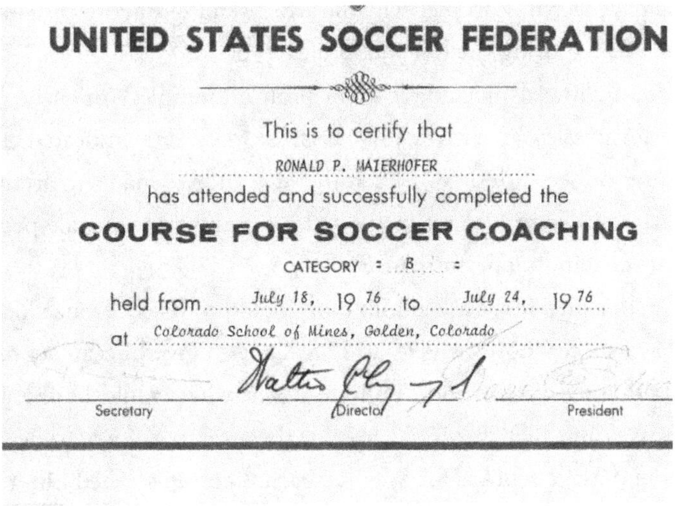
UNITED STATES SOCCER FEDERATION

This is to certify that

RONALD P. MAIERHOFER

has attended and successfully completed the

COURSE FOR SOCCER COACHING

CATEGORY : B :

held from July 18, 19 76 to July 24, 19 76

at Colorado School of Mines, Golden, Colorado

Secretary — Director — President

Figure 62
National "B" Coaching License 1976

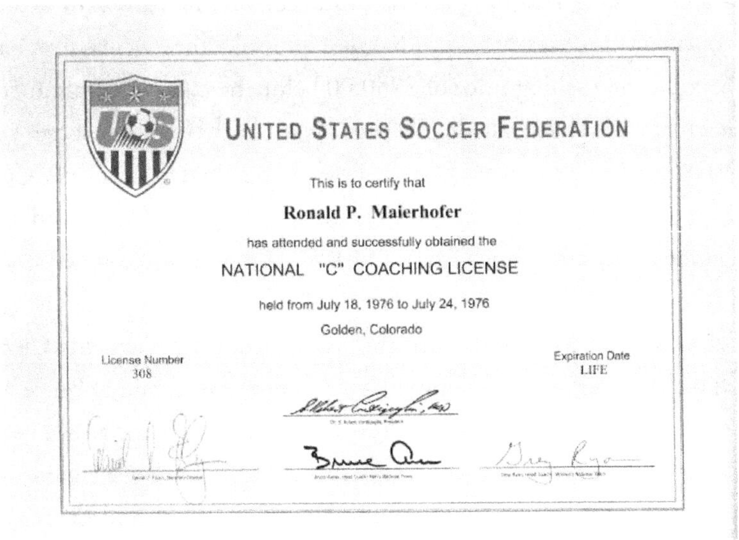
UNITED STATES SOCCER FEDERATION

This is to certify that

Ronald P. Maierhofer

has attended and successfully obtained the

NATIONAL "C" COACHING LICENSE

held from July 18, 1976 to July 24, 1976

Golden, Colorado

License Number 308

Expiration Date LIFE

Figure 63
National "C" Coaching License 1976

Pele'

One morning in early 1978, I was sitting in my office. My secretary said a gentleman wanted to visit with me to discuss a sales incentive idea. I told her I would see him. The man was an artist and his specialty was lost wax bronze art. If you have seen any art pieces by the artist Remington, they usually would have been created using the lost wax bronze process.

The artist showed me several small bronze examples which he believed could be great sales incentives for our sales force. He indicated he could produce any subject I desired. I liked the idea and we made an arrangement for him to produce bronze art pieces to be presented to our salespeople as a reward for outstanding performance.

During this meeting, I asked him if he could produce a bronze for me. He said yes! My soccer idol was Pele' so I arranged to give him an action photo of Pele' and asked if he could duplicate it and what would be the cost? He responded yes and that the initial cost for the artist proof would be $750.00 and he would make replicas for $300.00 each. I commissioned him to do the bronze but requested that he include two artist proofs in the deal. I suggested that he create a limited edition of twenty-five bronzes plus the two artist proofs and he agreed to my proposal. Additionally, he agreed to break the mold once the bronzes were produced. I pre-sold the twenty-five limited edition copies at a selling price of $750.00 before he completed production.

Later that year, The Colorado Caribous of the North American Soccer League (NASL) played its first game in Denver. Pele', who retired from the NY Cosmos in 1977, was a guest of the Caribous for that inaugural game. Dan Wood was the coach of the team at the time. Dan was a fellow Cornelian and coached Cornell's soccer team for five years during 1971-1975. He had been the assistant coach of the Caribous under the future Avalanche head coach, Dave Clements. Clements had left the team earlier in the season. Dan is famous for recruiting Bruce Arena, two-time US National Coach, to the Cornell soccer team. Bruce had been playing Lacrosse at Cornell as its goal keeper. The Caribous only lasted one year in Denver and were later purchased by Ted Turner, who moved the team to Atlanta where they became the Atlanta Chiefs of the NASL. Dan moved with the team and became head coach of the Atlanta Chiefs.

The Caribous had a press party after the inaugural game and I was introduced to Pele'. I showed Pele' a picture of the bronze we were having made. He graciously signed the picture shown below. I told him he would get the artist proof bronze from me on behalf of the kids playing soccer in Colorado.

When the artist delivered the artist proofs, I called the NY Cosmos office in New York City and arranged to meet with Pele' who was still in the United States. I indicated I wanted to present him with the bronze of himself on behalf of the children playing soccer in Colorado. He agreed to be available during one of my business trips to New York City. I hand-carried the thirty-two-pound bronze to the Denver Airport and onto the plane. I then took a cab to the Cosmos office and presented the bronze to him. He was very gracious and appreciative.

Figure 64
Bronze Statute of Pelé
NASL Caribous Game
1978

Figure 65
Finished Bronze of Pele'
Presented on Behalf of the
Children of Colorado 1978

Shortly after, I conceived the possibility of owning my own professional soccer team.

Chapter 10
Roars Indoors with the Denver Avalanche
1979-1983

It was now my time to consider being a sports team owner. This chapter contains excerpts from my first soccer book "No Money Down". It is my story about my three year ownership of the Denver Avalanche Indoor Soccer Team from 1979-1983. The book is available at most major online outlets. Below is Len Oliver's review of the book.

"No Money Down" — Good Soccer Read
Reviewed by Len Oliver, Director of Coaching
"Ron Maierhofer, former national team and pro player, and an old friend still active in our soccer world, has written an arresting tale of his adventure into owning a soccer franchise. Anyone who has ever dreamed of owning a sports franchise, or being involved in managing a pro team, should read and understand Maierhofer's experiences, or what he calls his "American Dream.

From 1979-1983, Maierhofer acquired and ran the Denver Avalanche, a professional indoor soccer franchise in the Major Indoor Soccer League (MISL). Maierhofer's book traces his personal odyssey through obtaining other people's money for a pro soccer team, outlining, chapter by chapter, his proven strategies for sports' marketing, making a game plan, enticing investors, and leaping legal hurdles along the way. Maierhofer offers the reader detailed insights into how a pro soccer franchise works, including staffing, marketing, obtaining players, and playing the game! He discusses the arcane topic of obtaining media coverage for pro soccer, with personal anecdotes that make the book come alive for the reader!

Maierhofer eventually loses the Denver Avalanche franchise in 1983, going into Chapter 11 bankruptcy and marking the end of his dream. But in conveying his personal journey through this informative soccer book, Maierhofer keeps the dream alive for others with a similar bent to own a soccer team, showing the rewards of contributing to our sport but also the pitfalls when soccer people become entrepreneurs. Maierhofer's story, so graphically written for us, reminds me of that old soccer saying, "We didn't lose, and we just ran out of time while being a goal down!"

Maierhofer remains in youth soccer through his firm, Sports Club Management, LLC, a national company providing soccer enrichment and online learning programs to young children under the name "KinderKickIt." Maierhofer's three sons have picked up the torch and continue their father's dream!" – By Len Oliver, Director of Coaching, DC Stoddert Soccer – Posted 12/15/09.

Excerpts from "No Money Down"

Birth of a Dream, 1979

Virgin Gorda is a beautiful, quiet island in the Caribbean. The island is part of the British Virgin Islands and not far from St. Thomas. It is conducive to introspective thought without interruptions from radio, television, newspapers, or telephones. My wife, Barb and I were vacationing in December 1979 from the annual rigors of orchestrating sales and marketing for Information Handling Services (IHS).

IHS was the information technology division of Indianhead, which was owned by the Dutch-based holding company, Thyssen Bornemisza.

Indianhead, headquartered in New York City, had fifty-one divisions. Today, IHS is a public company with over twenty billion dollars in sales. Back then, I was its Vice President of Operations after having been its Vice President of Sales and Marketing.

Earlier in December, I held a sales meeting at Disney World, Orlando Florida. We flew to Virgin Gorda after the meeting ended. I was forty-five years old and felt the need to make a change in my career. Perhaps the lunacy of owning a professional sports franchise was appropriate. My wife supported my intense feeling.

Up to that point, life had been good to us. We had four great sons, Scott, Jeff, Tim and Craig, and my business career was going well. We were making excellent money and had a relatively stable lifestyle. Yet, I seemed to be asking myself the question, "Do I really want to do this the rest of my life?" Barb and I talked about it for many hours while enjoying the peace, tranquility and panoramic beauty of the island.

Many men yearn to be a professional athlete and want the perceived glory that is associated with it. They also yearn for that elusive experience, often referred to as "fifteen minutes in the sun." I had experienced similar glory when I had been selected as a member of the USA National Soccer Team and participated in the Third Pan-American Games. However, I did not feel compelled to dream about owning a professional sports franchise because of I had underachieved in my own athletic career.

Friends would comment that I wanted a soccer franchise because of my love of the game. Rather, my business career had lost the exciting edge of the earlier years and I wanted to try something new. Because IHS was a software and data content company, it helped shape my view of sports. I always viewed professional sports from a programmer's point of view. To me, sports were software programs that perfectly suited television and other electronic media and soccer was included in that view. Looking back, this was a radical, forward thinking view of sports programming. The industry had not yet shaped its view of sports products as software events. Because it was the early years of cable television, sports programming was limited in its availability. ESPN had just started operations in the late 70's.

The birth of my dream really went back to my ethnic upbringing. As I indicated earlier, my parents were immigrants from Germany and arrived in the United States during the 1920's. History shows us that there was tremendous inflation in Europe at that time. Food and shelter were difficult to find and afford. Many Europeans, along with my mom and dad, chose to leave their homeland and seek new dreams in the United States. Mom and Dad also had a dream of a new life and felt America was the land of opportunity. While neither of them was highly educated, they took the risk of leaving their origins and starting that new life with the belief that there was opportunity in America.

My parents were strongly committed to the American dream. They believed that whatever you wanted, when combined with hard work, opportunity and a little bit of luck, you could achieve. My dad worked three jobs during the Depression and supported several families. As I was growing up, dreaming was part of reality. When I reflected on this basic philosophy shared by many of these immigrants to our country, I realized it was a powerful self-motivator for me but it was not enough. I soon came to understand this as I entered the world of the rich and powerful. Unfortunately, they didn't think that way!

During that vacation on Virgin Gorda, Barb and I reflected, agonized for several days and decided to make a critical move. For a number of years, I had been subscribing to a soccer magazine, *Soccer America*. It was founded by Clay Berling in 1967 and called Soccer West. Clay renamed the magazine Soccer America in 1972 and made it a weekly. While reading the magazine, I learned of a new and fascinating professional sport, indoor soccer, and its new league, the Major Indoor Soccer League. I knew nothing about this new sport or the new league, but I decided that when we returned to our home in Denver, I would explore the possibilities of owning a franchise with this league. Reflecting on this naïveté, I have often wondered what convinced me that I could be part of the sport's establishment. Ignorance is bliss!

Our family was comfortable and reasonably secure at this time. Most of our income and resources were being spent to raise a family and enjoying brief respites from the stresses of working hard. Certainly, no discretionary money was available to fund and operate a professional sports franchise, even if one were available. What a crazy idea! Perhaps dreaming and being naïve go hand-in-hand and help to make the impossible only take a little longer to achieve.

When we left the beautiful island of Virgin Gorda in December 1979, I was looking forward to making my fantasy dream come true. We decided I would remain at my job at and spend my spare time trying to "make it happen."

I now had to develop a "game plan." Have you ever tried to start or buy a professional franchise with no money down? Today, we are a society of instant communication. Often, we read and watch sports but never give a thought as to how our favorite franchise came into existence. How do you go about it? Is it possible? I believe that what you imagine is possible!

The Game Plan and Dream Award

The holidays soon ended and my improbable game plan began to take shape. In 1979, professional soccer in the United States had more than one league. The three major ones were the North American Soccer League (NASL), the American Soccer League (ASL) and the Major Indoor Soccer League (MISL). The Major Soccer League was to come much later.

The MISL concept developed out of an unsuccessful attempt to play indoor box lacrosse. Ed Tepper, a real estate developer in Philadelphia, started the league in 1978. He convinced several arena owners in major cities, including New York, Cleveland, Cincinnati, Philadelphia and Pittsburgh each to loan the league money to get started. These owners hoped to increase their winter revenue by hosting professional indoor soccer teams.

In 1978, Ed Tepper arranged for a Russian soccer team to visit the United States and play an outdoor game in Philadelphia. Terrific rains occurred during the week of the scheduled game and it had to be moved indoors. The game was a great success and Tepper modified the MISL rules to suit an indoor arena and television. Media reports speculated that the NASL was playing indoors to ward off competition from the new MISL.

Figure 66
MISL Brochure Cover 1980
Rocky Mountain News, November 16, 1980

By the fall of 1980, the MISL was prospering and growing. Its teams included: The St. Louis Steamers, partly owned by Baseball Hall of Famer, Stan Musial; the New York Arrows, owned by John Luciani, a major real estate developer and plastics manufacturing company owner in New Jersey; the Philadelphia Fever, owned by Ben Alexander, a relative of Earl Foreman, the MISL Commissioner; the Baltimore Blast; owned by Bernie Roden and later owned by Reds Scherer. Reds had a winner in the Preakness Horse Race; The Detroit Lightning, which was moved to San Francisco and became the Fog; the Hartford Hellions; the Cleveland Force, owned by Bert Wolstein, a real estate mogul, and nationally known as a developer of major shopping centers; the Chicago Horizon, owned by commercial real estate developer, Lee Stern; the Buffalo Stallions owned by Mike Geraci, Armand Castellani and principals of a major food market chain; the Wichita Wings, owned by Pizza Hut founders, brothers Dan and Frank Carney. It was later owned by Bill Kentling; the Phoenix Inferno, owned by Rick Ragone, another sports entrepreneur. Rick had been in the offices of the Miami Dolphins of the NFL, and General Manager of an NASL Soccer Franchise. He owned five antique car dealerships in Miami. He teamed with Rich Their of the Pfeiffer Salad Dressing empire to acquire the Phoenix franchise; and the San Francisco Fog, owned by real estate developer David Schoenstadt, who was also a former anesthesiologist.

Commissioner Earl Foreman, and Deputy Commissioner Ed Tepper, also had strong backgrounds in real estate and professional sports. Ed had been the President of the Philadelphia Atoms of the NASL. He made his money as a major real estate developer in the Philadelphia area. Earl, an attorney, was a former owner of the NFL's Philadelphia Eagles, the Baltimore Bullets of the NBA and the Washington Diplomats of the NASL.

The concept of the MISL was best captured in *Venture, The 'Magazine for Entrepreneurs'* in its April 1981 Soccer, American-Style article about the league, "The idea was to invent a form of soccer that would sell in the United States and what Tepper and Foreman developed was a game combining elements of hockey and pinball as well as outdoor soccer. The game is played in four 15-minute quarters on a 200-ft long by 85-foot wide field covered with artificial turf. The bright red leather ball ricochets off walls and bodies pinball fashion, speeding up the action of the game. As in hockey, penalties allow short-handed goal attempts and substitution of players. With only five players plus the goalie on field for each team, the ball keeps moving."

"We felt the game had to work on TV," said Tepper in the same article, noting the league had a national game of the week on the USA cable network. "We decided to use a red ball because it bleeds on television. We went with two halves and four quarters with timeouts to make room for commercial breaks. We constructed a higher goal to bring the action of the head-shot and scissors-kick back into the game. One of the big problems with outdoor soccer is that you can sit there all afternoon and see a 0-0 tie. We wanted 12 goals a game and we have been right on target."

"We're more interested in providing entertainment than pure sport [. . .]" Tepper continued. "The MISL requires a team to have thirteen North Americans on a sixteen player roster. Americans want to see Americans."

Tepper elaborated, "Also, most U.S. players, anxious for the chance to play, come cheaper at $25,000 per year or less versus hundreds of thousands of dollars for established, world-class foreign stars."

The NASL and the MISL soon competed against each other nationally. In some markets, they competed directly, although in 1983, they merged their indoor teams. I was aware of the competitive battles developing between these two leagues and that knowledge became part of my strategy as I developed my game plan. My first action would be to acquire rights to the arena. This would strengthen the application to either league and enhance my case to win a franchise award.

Indoor soccer is played within the confines of a hockey rink or basketball court. A green indoor artificial turf is placed either directly over the hockey-playing surface or over the basketball court floor. Denver had two professional sports teams that played games during the winter months. The Colorado Rockies were members of the National Hockey League (NHL). The league moved it to New Jersey in 1980 and it became the New Jersey Devils. The Denver Nuggets were members of the National Basketball League (NBA) and also played in the winter. Both teams played their home games in McNichols Arena, which has since been demolished and replaced by the Pepsi Center.

There were open playing dates in the schedules of both teams, which could provide scheduling opportunities for a professional indoor soccer team. How was I going to get the city officials to agree to make either arena available to a soccer team, especially when I had no money or other assets to guarantee any playing dates?

I evaluated both available arenas and decided that the major and larger McNichols Arena would offer the best opportunity to grow brand awareness and success. If my plan were to succeed at all, our team would have to play its games in a first class arena. Retrospectively, this was the first of a number of tough, questionable decisions, which were not so obvious to me at the time.

Figure 67
McNichols Arena 1980-1981
Denver Avalanche

During this period, I was becoming more involved in international trade. Its President, E.M. (Ted) Lee had managed to attract the former Governor of Colorado, Steve McNichols, to the company as an international consultant. Steve was working with the U.S. Department of Commerce at the time and was focusing on developing foreign trade for Colorado companies. You guessed it! Steve was the brother of Bill McNichols, Denver's Mayor.

I called Steve McNichols in early January of 1980 and discussed my dream with him. He thought another professional sports franchise, especially soccer, would be great for the City of Denver. Steve suggested that he should initiate a talk with Joe Nigro, a former state executive who worked for Steve while he was governor. Joe was the former Director of Public Utilities for the State of Colorado and was an attorney in Denver.

Wanting to remain in the background, Steve called me back a few days later and suggested I call Joe to arrange a face-to-face meeting with him to discuss a strategy to get the city officials on my side. Steve had previously indicated Joe was well connected with the City. I immediately called Joe, briefed him about my conversation with Steve, and arranged to meet the following evening for cocktails at the Denver Athletic Club.

Joe was a wonderful man and grandfather who had a low-key approach to life. We immediately clicked, and he too became excited about the prospects of another professional franchise in Denver. He was particularly excited because his grandchildren were playing soccer. Joe left the meeting that evening indicating he would make some inquiries as to the City's posture about leasing the McNichols Arena for indoor soccer. I didn't know at the time that those informal inquiries took place between Joe and Mayor Bill McNichols at the Mayor's home. I now know all dreams have to be assisted by those who can help make them happen!

A few days later, Joe called me and asked if I would like to join him for an exploratory meeting with Denver's facility officials. I was elated at the possibility and could not wait for the meeting to take place. A week later, Joe and I had lunch and reviewed our game plan before meeting at City Hall with the facility officials. The city officials were genuinely excited about the prospect of another professional team, and especially about the possibility of having another "long term" tenant in McNichols Arena. At this meeting, another stroke of luck occurred. Fred Luetzen, the General Manager of McNichols Arena, also attended. He was a German immigrant who loved soccer, and his children were playing it too.

The facility officials listened to my short presentation and obviously were primed to react positively. Joe then went to the heart of the matter and asked the City to give me an exclusive option on the arena for a professional indoor soccer franchise. I had specifically suggested to Joe, in our preliminary meetings, that the option not specify which league. I felt having a league name in the option would restrict my negotiating ability with either the MISL or the NASL. This turned out be one of the defining moments in the "game plan," and successfully positioned me to be granted a franchise from either league.

Several days later, Joe called me to give me the great news. He had been successful in getting the city officials to write a letter giving me the exclusive option to negotiate a lease. The lease would be for professional indoor soccer within the City of Denver. It specifically confirmed that the games would be played in McNichols Arena. The option was based on my being awarded a professional indoor soccer franchise for Denver. Wow, I now had letter from the City giving me exclusive rights to field a team for indoor soccer. The first play of my game plan was a home run!

I had negotiated the exclusive option less than a month after returning from our vacation. So far, my out-of-pocket costs were for cocktails, dinner and lunch. What was my next step? Money! I decided to contact my brother, Howard (Howie) Maierhofer, who was a stockbroker and investment banker in San Francisco, to ask him if he wanted to be involved.

HOWARD L. MAIERHOFER
General Partner and Owner

Figure 68
Howard Maierhofer
General Partner and Owner

Howie had a great love for soccer, and since the early 1960s had made many friends within the San Francisco financial community. He enthusiastically said 'yes' and indicated he would also talk to a number of close friends about investing. I told him I would contact the MISL about a possible franchise for Denver.

I telephoned Ed Tepper, the Deputy Commissioner of the MISL in Philadelphia. I with him my business and soccer background over the phone, and told him I had a group that was interested in a MISL franchise for the City of Denver. I explained that Denver could be a great franchise city for the league.

Tepper told me that the total franchise fee was $500,000. A deposit of at least $100,000 was required to make an application. Should we be awarded the franchise, the $100,000 deposit would be the minimum down payment due upon being awarded the franchise. Another criterion was that the applicant group had to have a substantial net worth. He reiterated that Denver was a very desirable franchise city and that a number of similar "groups" from Denver had also contacted him and shown strong interest. I again gave him my background and asked for a meeting with him and Earl Foreman. Ed came across as somewhat hesitant – so I unloaded the bomb on him!

During that call, I told Tepper that I had an exclusive written option from the City of Denver to use its major arena, McNichols Arena, for hosting games for a professional soccer franchise. I told him that the NASL had also expressed strong interest in Denver. I implied that if the MISL were not interested in my application, we would apply to the NASL. Tepper quickly changed his attitude and suggested we make immediate application to the MISL and the board of directors would strongly consider Denver as an expansion franchise for the next season (1980-81). My strategy had worked!

Now I had a place to play professional indoor soccer, and the MISL was showing strong interest. Still, I had no significant liquid net worth, financial partners or money. And, I needed the $100,000 deposit immediately!

Later that night, I called Howie and updated him on my conversation with Tepper. Neither one of us had that kind of ready cash, but Howie, a San Francisco Stock Broker at the time, offered a suggestion. He had friends who could easily handle the $100,000 deposit in return for an equal share of the equity in the franchise. Howie said he would present the idea to several of them that night to determine their interest.

The next day, Howie called me back and confirmed that several of his friends were definitely interested. The MISL had a franchise in San Francisco at the time. It was named the "Fog," and played its games at the Cow Palace. Howie believed there could be substantial financial interest from other friends in the bay area.

The following week, Howie called back and asked if he and a friend could meet with me in Denver. We arranged to meet at the Regency Hotel in North Denver, near McNichols Arena. I had never been personally involved with an investment of this magnitude and could barely sleep waiting for the day of the meeting. When the day arrived, I could not focus at work and anxiously waited for lunchtime.

I met Howie and his friend, and we chatted about the opportunity. Finally, the friend agreed he would front the $100,000 down payment required with the submission of the application to the MISL. He suggested the three of us form a General Partnership. He was familiar with this entity management form because of his real estate deals. After our application was awarded, we would then raise operational funds from other investors. Once we were granted the franchise, he felt we should try to raise approximately $2.0 million to fund our first few years. He was familiar with an investment vehicle known as a Limited Partnership. He was involved in a number of these offerings with personal friends of his. Those investors could be limited partners, and the three of us would be the general partners.

After receiving our funding, we agreed that the Limited Partnership would pay the friend back his $100,000 for the franchise application down payment. In return for fronting the down payment and submitting his financial statement, his friend would receive one third of the General Partnership. The General Partnership would retain 50% of the Limited Partnership after raising $2.0 million from private investors, who would become limited partners.

This was my first real exposure to the concept of OPM (Other People's

Money), and I was excited. However, I did not fully understand the Golden Rule: those with the gold, rule!

Howie felt I should be the Managing General Partner and spearhead the application process. Since I lived in Denver, I volunteered to do the initial work. However, we would have to decide on my role should we be awarded the franchise. We decided that I would resign and run the franchise on a day-to-day basis. We agreed to determine the details later.

The next step in my game plan was to create the illusion that our group had substance and desirability. I made calls to friends and acquaintances whose business credentials I felt would impress the MISL board of directors. They were chosen for a variety of team building reasons: soccer background, business acumen, television or cable background, marketing background, and their financial balance sheet. I then created a Board of Advisors for the sole purpose of making the application to the MISL. I contacted several of them, and all agreed we could use their names and resumes on the application.

Several days later, I completed the application form, and with the deposit check for $100,000, submitted our application to the MISL league office. Ed Tepper called me shortly after receiving the application and told me that the league was having its annual board of directors meeting in St. Louis on February 27, 1980. He asked if our group would be interested in being guests at the MISL's first All-Star Game, its showcase event. I said that we would be thrilled. And, hopefully we could get a positive answer on our application.

Tepper indicated that the league board of directors would be voting on the Denver applications at the All-Star Game and that representatives from several other cities in which the league was interested would also attend. I mentally noted he implied several groups were making applications." At any rate, I said we would be delighted to attend the game and were expecting to be awarded a franchise. Wow – were we getting any closer?

We flew into St. Louis the morning of February 27, 1980. When we arrived at the hotel, we were told that the league's board of directors was meeting. I did not know it at the time, but Stan Musial, a member of the Baseball Hall of Fame, was on the league board. He and his group were the owners of the league's most successful franchise, the St. Louis Steamers. The

Steamers were averaging 12,000 fans per game. We also discovered that Cincinnati's franchise had been owned by the infamous Pete Rose, another baseball legend, and the franchise later closed after its first season. I was impressed and hoped we could become part of this league. We sat for several hours in the lobby of the hotel awaiting the application decision. The time had come to determine the status of my dream!

Shortly after lunch, we were called into the meeting. At the time, we did not know that the owners and team officials of the Denver Zephyrs, a minor league baseball franchise, were also there waiting for a decision on their application. We joined the board meeting and Earl Foreman introduced us. Earl nonchalantly said "Welcome to the league." We had arrived! We had been awarded the franchise and the first phase of the dream was now real. Amazingly, it took only about two months to accomplish.

Figure 69
Welcomed to the MISL by Stan Musial
St. Louis Steamers Game 1980

We saw our first professional indoor soccer game that night. What a night to celebrate! The Steamers had a full house for the MISL's first All Star Game – 16,892 raucous fans. We were hooked! We left St. Louis the next morning, high in hopes and wondering how we were going to raise $2.0 million in operating capital we estimated we needed to sustain the franchise for the next several years.

I would soon be enmeshed in that wonderful entrepreneurial world, the world of taxation and venture capitalism. The dream had become reality. We had a long way to go to get operational, but we certainly had made great progress towards its fruition.

Figure 70
MISL Game, 1980 MISL Marketing

Marketing the Dream! A Vision Ahead of its Time

When I was a little boy, I wanted to be both a soccer player and a clown! By starting this franchise, I accomplished both. Today, it is difficult for younger people to visualize what professional sports resembled in the late 1970s and early 1980s. Cable TV was in its infancy and we had no regional sports networks. In retrospect, attending a game was an exercise in watching players and vocally reacting to their plays. The games were all viewed as competitive events, not as entertainment.

The fans were predominantly male adults. Nationally, there were three major professional sports: baseball (MLB), basketball (NBA) and football (NFL), all played by men. Tennis was the only female sport of consequence shown on television. Hockey (NHL), the fourth major professional sport, had great fan attendance in selected cities, but a poor television following. In some cities, two professional winter sports teams were competing for the same sports dollar – basketball and hockey.

The MISL emerged from this sports crucible. Right from its inception, the founders viewed their infant league as entertainment; being a sport was secondary. The league founders were visionary and designed their product to be viewed on television. The MISL used reddish-orange balls, mascots and cheerleaders to provide pizzazz to the quick-action, high-scoring show time events. The fans were thunderous in response to the presentation of the game by the teams.

The marketing managers of each of the teams were also visionary and ahead of their time. Many of these marketing leaders, like the Leiweke Brothers, later saw their careers escalate in established sports leagues and teams. Many sports celebrities endorsed the new league as evidenced by the following quotes at the time.

"You see one game and you're hooked. I saw one game and I bought a team in the MISL – What a great business opportunity – I love it." **Stan Musial, MLB Hall of Famer**

"I first went to soccer games when I was in high school, in the 1930s. . . So I had a great liking for soccer for 40, almost 50 years . . . and I continue to be fascinated." **Howard Cosell**

"Indoor soccer is the most exciting sport I've seen and soccer has become my second love. Indoor soccer gives the fans what they want — speed, scoring and hustle." **Pete Rose**

"I think soccer, more so than any other sport, aside from tennis and volleyball, lends itself to letting women become professionals. There's a strength factor in other sports that prevents them from competing with men, but in soccer the most important tools are quickness and endurance." **Earl "The Pearl" Monroe, NBA Hall of Famer**

Figure 71
Avalanche Fan
Earl "The Pearl" Monroe

I had a strong background in marketing and considered this opportunity a marketer's dream! The thought of introducing a new product to new fans in a new city was an opportunistic challenge. It is said, "Opportunity is a good chance that always looks bigger going than coming." I felt the opposite, and viewed the opportunity to succeed as probable, not impossible!

Some people later viewed our franchise accomplishments as a miracle. Peter Drucker said, "Miracles are great, but they are so damned unpredictable." We now had to roll up our sleeves and "make it happen!" In addition, we had to approach the marketing opportunity as if it were like any other product introduction challenge in the business world. I viewed myself as a rare owner in the league. I was a day-to-day franchise leader, a former player and, by profession, a marketing professional.

I met with the new staff and posed a challenge to them: Define the business we are in and list the steps we would have to take to implement what was now "our dream?" We concluded, after several days and evenings of intensive planning and schmoozing, we were not in the soccer business, but rather, in the entertainment business. The league's philosophy became our philosophy, and entertainment became our strategic positioning. This thought shaped all our marketing strategies, day-of-game activities and tactics.

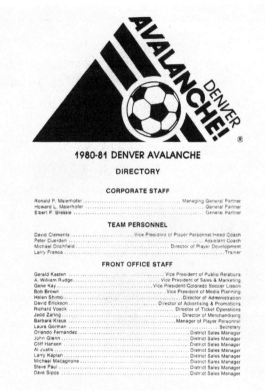

Figure 72
Avalanche Staff Directory
1980-1981

We decided to first name the team as our course of action. Secondly, we needed to understand who our potential fans were. Then, we would develop marketing plans to convince those prospects to try our product.

Naming the Team

When we first announced that we had been awarded a franchise for the City of Denver, we received terrific publicity in the local newspapers. We also announced that our new product would be introduced in the fall of 1980.

The staff collectively decided that we would have a name-the-team contest.

Initially, we did not realize the power of our strategy. It helped launch us as a marketing force to be reckoned with in Denver! We created newspaper advertisements for the major newspapers, the *Denver Post* and the *Rocky Mountain News*. Then we contacted all the major radio stations to arrange a number of airtime interviews. At the time, Denver was one of the radio-station leaders in the country. Over thirty-five radio stations were headquartered in the area. In addition, we contacted all the local soccer organizations and asked them to help us name the team. They were also thrilled to participate. The contest ran for two weeks in early summer.

We were shocked and amazed by the response to the contest. We had over twenty-one hundred contestants. My sons, Scott, Jeff, Tim and Craig spent hours just opening the envelopes from the respondents. As one would expect, many of the submitted names were repeated and predictable. However, one name surfaced immediately. The staff loved it! It had been submitted by a young girl named Donna Vullmer. She submitted "Avalanche" and the rest is history. Donna was eleven years old and a sixth-grade student at Red Rocks School in Morrison, Colorado. She and four members of her immediate family received a trip to Mexico for winning the contest.

Denver Avalanche General Partners congratulate Donna Vullmer, winner of the name the team contest.

Figure 73
Winner Name the Team Contest
Donna Vullmer 1980 Denver Avalanche

It was a big event when we announced the winning contestant and the new team name. We received wonderful press. A local graphic artist was asked to draw several logos reflecting the name, and what it meant in Colorado. Below is the Avalanche logo, showing the predominant colors of the State of Colorado: blue for the sky, white for the snow, and green for the mountains. The angle of the logo symbolized skiing, the predominant winter sport in Colorado. We added a soccer ball. We were now in business. We had a moniker and a logo we could market!

Figure 74
Avalanche Logo April, 1980

Demographics Shape the Dream

Concurrent with the naming of the franchise, we had to determine our fan demographics. Howie indicated he knew of a highly regarded sport consulting firm headquartered in the San Francisco area and suggested I contact it. Its name was Pacific Select and it was owned by Matt Levine.

Matt brought relevant sports and entertainment experience to the franchise. He was an innovative and energetic senior level marketing executive and leader, who's strong branding capabilities earned him prominence in sports and entertainment.

Levine had also been a keynote speaker at national meetings of the MLB, NBA, NHL, the NFL and many other sports conferences. He was well connected with many sports leaders, owners and national companies that spent advertising dollars in sports.

Furthermore, Levine had been featured in the *New York Times*, *Wall Street Journal*, *Time*, *Newsweek*, and Sports *Illustrated* and on major television and cable networks for breakthrough innovations in branding, licensing, introduction of consumer marketing practices, event staging and technology in sports and entertainment industries. Pacific Select was renowned for its sports marketing research.

The traditional fans for major sports in the early 1980s were men, predominantly in the twenty-one to thirty-five demographic age brackets. Clearly, we would have great difficulty in trying to entice them away from basketball or hockey.

I met with Matt and decided to fund a market research study. Its objective was to determine the potential demographic markets for indoor soccer. Normally, in the private sector, we would have conducted this market research before we made the decision to buy the franchise rights. We had moved rapidly since February 1980, and now wanted to ensure that we directed our marketing message to the right demographic slices.

Several weeks later, Matt presented us with the results of Pacific Select's market research study and the results were stunning. The study showed only 23% of the attendance at an NBA game was female. The NHL's percentage of female fans attending its games was even lower. In addition, the percentage of attendance of youth or families at both these pro sporting events was even lower than the percentage of females. Pacific Select also determined that females were more inclined to attend professional sporting events when they could view the body in motion.

Our new "Denver Avalanche" indoor soccer team presented a wonderful opportunity to market to and attract a fan base that was relatively new to professional sports – women! The players on the pro indoor soccer teams were young, athletic and generally attractive. And, they wore simple uniforms which showed their bodies. Women were not inclined to watch the violent nature of sports like hockey and football. We believed females would watch young athletic players and identify with them. They also wanted to be entertained. The study strongly recommended that we focus on marketing to the female demographics.

Figure 75
Advertisement – Scream and Shout,
Rocky Mountain News October 16, 1980

Additionally, the Pacific Select study concluded that we had a prime opportunity to attract the demographic "family" market. Major professional sports had been unsuccessful at penetrating this market. The high cost of tickets, food and drink while at major sporting events prevented winter pro sports teams from attracting the family-oriented fan. Soccer, at that time, was the dominant growth sport in the United States. The study concluded that creative "family oriented" pricing of tickets at the arena would appeal to those potential fans and give us an advantage.

The study's conclusions became the basis for our marketing strategies and shaped the creation of our supporting marketing materials. The decision to market to females and families would become our singular most important strategy. It was designed to create marketing success for the new franchise.

The conclusion of the first season reinforced our marketing strategy. That first season, 47% of our fans were female. This attendance was unheard of in professional sports. Also, we were able to capture a significant share of the twenty-one to thirty-five age segments, which we first thought unrealistic. Forty-seven percent of our fans were in that "hard to reach" eighteen to thirty-four age range. Our research had indicated that the typical soccer household was four members. The average U.S. household in 1980 was 2.9 members. The average family purchased four tickets to a game, which confirmed that we were appealing to the young family. Our marketing strategy was working!

FAMILY INCOME LEVELS

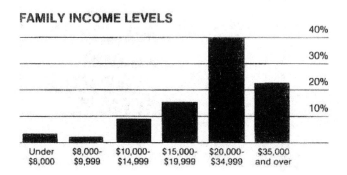

| Under $8,000 | $8,000-$9,999 | $10,000-$14,999 | $15,000-$19,999 | $20,000-$34,999 | $35,000 and over |

Soccer Fans as Consumers of Packaged Goods

	Frequency Among Buyers Total US				
	Bought In Past Month	One or more a day	One or more a week	2-3 times a month	Once a month
Coffee	77%	25%	26%	24%	25%
Tea	57	15	29	25	31
Soda pop/soft drinks	80	24	50	19	7
Beer	65	17	38	27	18
Wine	50	8	28	33	30
Whisky type liquor	40	9	19	27	45
White type liquor	33	8	19	26	47
Cigarettes	39	36	43	14	8
Cigars	13	19	25	17	39
Fast food items	78	8	39	35	17
Snack foods	73	14	52	25	10
Candy	63	13	48	26	12
Gum	64	15	47	26	12

*SOURCE: TCA, INC., 500 Fifth Ave., New York, N.Y. 10036

Figure 76
Game Demographics 1980-81
Denver Avalanche

Pricing the Dream Product

Immediately after receiving the Pacific Select report, I called a meeting of the staff with the purpose of discussing how we could implement its suggestions. The staff concurred we would market to women and families, and that each demographic target market presented its own set of tactics. The staff's first priority was to address the pricing of tickets. We wanted to attract these two major target markets, but we first had to make it easy.

Our pricing was to be designed to allow families to afford and attend our games. Once they were at the game, we would entertain them. We hoped that they left raving about the great time they had at the game. We wanted them to return, shouting for more. The staff was convinced we could win these two demographic targets when pitted against the other winter professional sports teams.

Will Rogers once commented, "Even if you're on the right track, you'll get run over if you just sit there." We had to do something extraordinary to win over these market targets. Since our season opened in ninety days, the strategy had to be put into practice quickly. The configuration of the arena for indoor soccer and hockey was to prove the answer to our dilemma.

The pro basketball court in the McNichols Arena was configured like most indoor arenas around the country that also hosted a professional hockey team. The basketball court was placed over the sheet of ice every time the Nuggets played. Conversely, when the Rockies pro hockey team played, its ice surface was narrower than the basketball court. As a result, when the Rockies played its games, the stadium personnel put temporary seating between the permanent seating and the hockey dasher boards. This collapsible temporary seating was about six rows deep and made of aluminum. When stomped on with feet, it made a monstrous noise! Branch Rickey, the Yankee's great manager, once said, "Luck is the residue of design." The collapsible aluminum seat stadium design blessed us and fortuitously separated us from the pro hockey and basketball teams.

We developed a pricing plan that revolutionized pro sports. The lowest ticket price was to be $4.40 including tax. The staff felt this price would induce families to participate. We also reversed the normal pricing concept for these cheapest seats. The lowest price in most arenas was for seating that was the least optimal for viewing, and generally the farthest from the action. Indoors, this was generally referred to as the "peanut gallery."

Figure 77
Children's World Schedule
1980-81 Denver Avalanche

Alternatively, we offered low-priced ringside tickets to children. These ringside seats were six rows deep and circled the dasher boards. We named it the "Rumble" section. Imagine hearing several thousand kids pounding on the dasher boards and on the aluminum seating with their feet! The Avalanche roared! And the sound was soon to become deafening!

Figure 78
Avalanche Roars Indoors

It was hoped, by panning the television cameras around the dashboards during a game, that we would be able to capture the excitement of the game for the home audience. This could induce more families to join in the fun by attending a live event. We felt sure we could not miss with this strategy.

We structured the remaining sections of the stadium seating to ensure we would continue to appeal to families. The Avalanche Patrol Loge seats were priced at $6.00 each; the Slide Watch Dress Circle Loge (center of the arena) was priced at $7.50; the Patrol House Corporate Box seats at $9.00; the Snow Cap Balcony seats at $5.00 each; and the Blue Sky Peanut Gallery at $3.00 per seat. The pricing structure was substantially lower than our competitors, the Denver Nuggets and the Colorado Rockies (now the New Jersey Devils of the NHL).

With our pricing, we did right by families! Mark Twain said, "Always do right. This will gratify some people and astonish the rest!" The Denver sports community was astonished at our pricing and flocked to buy our season ticket plans and our day-of-game, thirteen-game and six-game ticket packages.

Snow Cats! Sleek and Opulent

Again, another stroke of marketing luck came our way. During the summer of 1980, it was said by many that there were only two sports in Denver – the Denver Broncos during the season and the Denver Broncos in the off-season. The Broncos were owned by Edgar Kaiser, heir to Kaiser Industries and its collective companies. That summer, Kaiser fired the Bronco cheerleaders, which many in the NFL thought were equal to the fabled Dallas Cowboy Cheerleaders. Bad mistake!

A member of the Bronco cheerleaders was Debbie La Porta. She was dating Mike Ditchfield at the time, our newly hired Assistant Coach. Debbie called me shortly after it was announced that the Bronco cheerleaders had been disbanded by Kaiser. She asked if the Avalanche would be interested in adding them to our marketing team. She indicated that between twelve and twenty-two of the cheerleaders could be part of the Avalanche "mystique." I expressed my excitement about the idea and asked her to drop in the office to chat about it.

DEBBIE LaPORTA
Cheerleader Coordinator

Figure 79
Debbie La Porta
Cheerleader Coordinator, Denver Avalanche

Our marketing people went crazy when they heard about it and thought it would position us skillfully in the market. It would 'put us on the map and the community would associate us with the other major sports. Little did we know how true our prophecy would ring!

Debbie arrived the next day with several of her co-cheerleaders in tow. Not surprisingly, word got out to some of our players who were already signed. They unexpectedly showed up to meet the gorgeous, young, vibrant and full of energy young female cheerleaders. How could we not hire them? I told Debbie we were very interested, but that we had to watch our budget. What would they charge us? Debbie suggested, since the cheerleaders were now unemployed, a fee of $15 per game per lady would suffice. We agreed. Furthermore, they agreed to participate in our after-game parties at a local restaurant. In addition, they would get a free dinner and drinks at the after-game party restaurant. Debbie quickly agreed to all our terms, and suddenly, the Avalanche had a nationally recognized cheerleading team equal to any in the NFL. This was to be a marketing coup for the team and significantly helped launch our branding effort.

**1981-82
DENVER AVALANCHE
SNOW CATS**
Figure 80

Ultimately, twenty-one cheerleaders, including four young men, signed on to be part of the Avalanche's Snow Cats. We named Debbie our SnowCats Cheerleader Coordinator and crowned Kathleen Buell 'Miss Lady Avalanche.

The Marketing Department later arranged to take group photos of the ladies posing with several of our good- looking players. The color photos soon became a poster, and thousands were distributed to fans throughout the metro area. I would bet that many Denver area men still have those posters today!

When we made our announcement, we received tremendous media exposure. And, without realizing what we had accomplished, we were able to penetrate the eighteen to thirty-five male target market dominated by major professional sports that we had previously thought lost. Soon, young men would be flocking to the Avalanche games just to watch the Snow Cats. What an event to watch!

Partnering with the Dream Merchants

When I lived in the Dallas area in the early 1970s, I had an experience similar to the one with Surfco. Then, I had co-founded competitive youth soccer in the North Texas area. I convinced Dr. Pepper, a division of Coca Cola, to advertise with our newly founded youth travel league. As I recall, the advertisement branding investment by Dr. Pepper was among the first such advertising investments in youth soccer in the country. This experience, coupled with the Surfco experience and input from the other MISL franchises, became the basis for our strategic partnering strategy.

Armed with the Surfco success, the marketing department put together a strategic marketing package for potential sponsors. We believed a number of companies with Colorado marketing activities would similarly be second-class citizens with the other professional sports teams. They too, might be prevented from participating as sponsors with the three major professional sport franchises in Denver.

Forty-five days later, we had successfully signed nineteen strategic partnerships with companies like Coca Cola, McDonalds, Anheuser Bush, May D&F, Oracle Waterbed, Guaranty Bank, KPPL/KLAK Radio, Mammoth Garden, and others. All of these partnerships were based on co-marketing activities and used their retail leverage to promote relationships with the Avalanche. Additionally, they all purchased the Avalanche Club Season Ticket Packages. Each of them also helped defray many of the associated marketing costs of our launch efforts.

Figure 81
Budweiser Advertisement 1980-81

One example of these partnerships was with St. Louis- based Anheuser Bush. At that time, Anheuser Bush was one of the major companies advertising at the MISL level. It bought full pages in team media guides and in the *Missile,* the league's magazine, and did other co-marketing activities with the league. Its President, Denny Long was an avid soccer player and fan. He and Anheuser were totally committed to the league and, where possible, to supporting its franchises. The Avalanche's relationship with Anheuser Bush was to become one its strongest partnerships. However, it was not to come easily!

Figure 82
Missile Magazine Front Cover
Buffalo Stallions, November 14, 1980

I contacted Denny Long and asked him if he would be willing to agree to become a sponsor and participate in some marketing activities with the Avalanche. He said Anheuser Busch would normally be interested but that it had a problem in Denver. The company had been trying to get its products, which he characterized as beer "taps", into McNichols Arena since its opening and had not succeeded. Because of this, he felt Anheuser's involvement with the Avalanche could only be nominal. He suggested I contact Mike Roarty; his Vice President of Marketing, to see what could be done.

I contacted Mike and we met to discuss Anheuser's potential involvement. He reiterated their problem with "taps" in McNichols and felt it wouldn't make sense to co-market with or become a sponsor with the Avalanche. I asked him what commitment he would be willing to make in the way of joint activities or actual dollars if we could get taps in there. I felt we had an extra edge with the City and might be influential in having the stadium add some Anheuser Bush taps during the professional games of all the sports teams. He said that if we could assist getting taps into McNichols, they would sponsor the Avalanche and do some co-marketing with us. I then asked him if they would be willing to give us twelve minutes of paid advertising in our television games since we were preparing to buy our own time from Channel 2 WGN TV and produce our own game. He responded to my pre-closing question by saying, "Of course, we could do that!" But, I believe he strongly felt we would not be able to accomplish that and he said 'yes' to our request knowing he would not have to make his promise good.

I quickly discovered from the McNichols Arena officials that they did not make "beer tap" decisions. Instead, the decision had to be made by AraServe, from Philadelphia. A light bulb went off in my head at the time. "AraServe" sounded so familiar to me. Then I remembered, while I was growing up in Buffalo, New York, my father's accountant and I became very close. He was my mentor and influenced me when I began college to major in accounting, hoping that I would become a CPA like him. One of his major clients was the Jacob Brothers, who owned AraServe!

The Jacob Brothers were a huge success and owned a number of major league sport stadiums throughout the United States. Its service arm was AraServe, headquartered in Philadelphia. The Avalanche marketing staff had hired Larry Kaplan to be a young intern for the team. When I reviewed the Anheuser Busch situation with our marketing staff, Larry indicated he also had a strong relationship with AraServe. We contacted AraServe, and one day later, AraServe had given Anheuser Busch a tap within McNichols Arena. Another stroke of luck for the franchise!

Mike Roarty called me when he discovered they now had a tap at McNichols Arena and was ecstatic with our help! He wrote in his letter to me, "We certainly appreciate your efforts on our behalf at McNichols Arena. While we are not totally satisfied with the distribution of products in the stands, at least we have the door open thanks to you. Your cooperation on this matter was throughout, beyond the call of duty, and we appreciate it very much. Looking forward to seeing you soon." That day, Anheuser Bush committed to be the major sponsor for the Avalanche and assisted us with a number of marketing efforts, including our television strategy.

Carving the Huts – A Television Odyssey

Television can be the backbone to the success of every sports league. It is as valid today and as it was valid in the late 1970s and early 1980s. When the

Avalanche was first awarded its franchise, the league had a minor national television contract with the USA Network, an early entrant (1977) in the cable industry. USA Network was more dominant in televising sports than a new, upstart cable company, the Entertainment and Sports Programming Network, now known as ESPN (1979). USA Network was headed by its President, Kay Kopliwitz, and is currently owned by NBC Universal.

The first major national cable program was HBO in 1978. By 1980, cable television had grown to twenty-six national programs and served about fifteen million households. However, cable only had about a 9% share of the fifteen million Huts (Households under Television). The industry grew quickly during the Avalanche's brief history. For example, by 1985, cable had forty million subscribers. The years 1975-1985 were glorious years for the cable industry. Today, there are about one hundred and fifty million households among Cable, Netflix, Pay TV and Direct TV.

The Avalanche forged its electronic marketing strategy against this cable industry background. When we joined the league, it had a national contract with the USA Network for a MISL Game of the Week. The USA Network, in its infancy, only had about 1.3 million subscribers nationally. An even smaller percentage of these subscribers watched sports programs, and most did not watch indoor soccer. When it started, the Avalanche had no contract and had to develop a strategy to get its new programming in front of a larger television audience.

By 1978, a Chicago based television station WGN, had syndicated itself and became a superstation. Its Denver based affiliate, WGN of Denver, was an independent fourth television network player in the crowded Denver television market. The national networks included CBC, NBC and ABC. Shortly after we announced the franchise award, I contacted the four Denver television stations to inquire about coverage of our games. The major networks arbitrarily turned us down. WGN, an independent network, was interested, but took the position that they could not afford to produce our games. Instead, they suggested we consider producing our own games. Then, they would consider transmitting and covering our home games in prime time if we would buy the airtime. But, if we did decide to produce the games, we would have to fill the time we bought from them.

In 1980, the Denver Broncos was the only Denver sport franchise to have an affiliation with a national network. Both the Denver Nuggets and the Colorado Rockies were on the smaller independent, KWGN-TV Channel 2. However, neither franchise produced its own games. WGN covered and transmitted those games and sold the advertising. Denver is a unique location for the cable industry. It is one of the few cities in the United States geographically positioned to transmit a television signal nationally to both eastern and western locations with one single "bounce" or transmission. The ability to transmit directly considerably reduces the cost of programming distributed by any cable network. Denver became the early center of many of the national cable programming companies and they later became networks. We wanted to take advantage of the emerging cable industry to market to our demographics and penetrate those markets.

I reviewed the KWGN Channel 2 conversation with the marketing staff and after a lengthy and open discussion, it was decided that we would try to produce the games ourselves. I would be a challenge since neither Jerry Kasten nor I had any experience at doing this. By producing the games ourselves, we would have to control the broadcasting of the game, hire the announcers, create the surrounding vignettes around the game itself, and most importantly sell the advertising time within the game. I went back to KWGN-TV Channel 2 and told them we would commit to doing our home games and would buy the two-hour slots from them for each game. We had no idea of whether or not we could successfully sell the advertising, but plunged ahead anyway.

KWGN-TV Channel 2 sold its own time for the Nuggets and Rockies games. Typically, a thirty-second spot in a Nuggets basketball game cost between $500 and $800, depending on how the advertiser bought the time. The Rockies' television spots were from $300 to $700 depending on how time was purchased. The Avalanche decided to price a thirty-second spot at $750. We felt we could justify the higher spot cost by including promotional and merchandising support.

The media staff put together a television sponsorship package to support our television advertising. It included the television spots with four billboards per game; one at the beginning of the game; another at the end of the first half; one at the beginning of the second half; and one at the end of the game. It also included prominent positioning in the official media guide (Anheuser Bush got the inside cover) and season tickets priced at $8 per ticket.

During the inaugural 1980-81 season, the Avalanche aired ten games. Seven of those were road games and three were home games. The average cost to produce a game in prime time included $6000 for buying the time slot from Channel 2, $4,700 for satellite transmission charges, and $5,500 for production and on air talent. The total cost for a prime time game was $16,200.

The Avalanche was successful in adding two great announcers to its television staff. Jim Conrad was the Sports Director at KWGN-TV Channel 2 and agreed to do the play-by-play for us. Kyle Rote, Jr. agreed to do the color commentary. Kyle was also the color man for the MISL Game of the Week on the USA Cable Network.

Kyle was a fabulous choice. He and I played on the Dallas Rangers adult soccer team in the early 1970s. Kyle was about eighteen-years-old then and new to soccer. He was an outstanding athlete, and by the time he was twenty-one, he was playing soccer for the Dallas Tornado of the NASL. Coincidently, his father Kyle Rote, Sr. presented me with an athletic award while I attended Cornell University. Kyle Rote, Sr. played for the New York Giants and is a Hall of Fame member. Kyle Rote, Jr. was a great all-around athlete, and the only person ever to win ABC's Superstars competition three times, taking the title in 1974, 1976 and 1977. Both Jim and Kyle gave our television broadcast terrific credibility. We were the first to put together a regional sports network.

**1980-81
AVALANCHE TV SCHEDULE**

Jim Conrad   Kyle Rote Jr.

Ten Avalanche games this season will be televised over KWGN-TV, Channel 2 in Denver. The TV schedule includes three home games and seven road games. Televised games are scheduled as follows:

Fri., Nov. 14, 1980 .... Denver at Buffalo
Wed., Nov. 19, 1980 .... San Francisco at Denver
Wed., Dec. 3, 1980 ..., ... Hartford at Denver
Fri., Dec. 12, 1980 .... Denver at St. Louis
Fri., Jan. 2, 1981 .... Denver at New York
Wed., Jan. 21, 1981 .... Denver at Wichita
Thurs., Jan. 29, 1981 .... Denver at San Francisco
Sat., Feb. 14, 1981 .... Denver at Philadelphia
Fri., Feb. 20, 1981 .... Denver at St. Louis
Mon., Mar. 2, 1981 .... Chicago at Denver

Figure 83
Avalanche TV Staff and Schedule
1980-81

Sponsorships in the inaugural year included six minutes from Anheuser-Bush in each game at $1500 per minute for the season total of $90,000, two minutes in each game from May D&F equaling $30,000, and ninety-seconds from Oracle Waterbeds in some games ($9000). The balance of the advertisers were either trade accounts or spot buyers. They would buy one game at a time where it would fit into their overall television advertisement campaign.

The trade accounts were with KPPL/KLAK radio. They had one minute of trade time, as did our training facility, Mammoth Gardens. We averaged 11.5 minutes per game of advertising our first season. No effort was made to get extra spot sales once the season started. The prime time games drew an average 5% rating and an 8% share. These ratings were not equal to a national network station like CBS, which drew a 17% rating and a 28% share. However, as a fledgling sports franchise, it gave us great exposure in the market place, continued to reinforce our marketing message that we were the 'new kid on the block,' and could challenge the Nuggets and the Rockies.

By the end of our second season, we became strong enough to consummate a contract in the summer of 1982 with Denver's CBS affiliate, KMGH-TV and Channel 7. That contract would be the league's first contract with a national network. Neither the Nuggets nor the Rockies could make that claim. In the 1982-83 season, they remained on the smaller, local independent station, KWGN TV Channel 2. Our arrangement with CBS was the same as it had been with Channel 2.

The agreement with CBS for the 1982-83 season required a maximum of twenty games to be televised. Two of those games were committed to be prime time broadcasts between 6 and 10 p.m, with the remaining games scheduled on the weekend. The scheduling of the station and the league would determine which games were on Saturday or Sunday. It was projected that several of the games might have to be on tape delay. The cost of being on a national network was considerably higher than would have been on Channel 2. We raised our advertising rate to $2600 per minute and budgeted for twenty-three minutes of advertising per game. Alas, as events unfolded, we would never get to produce games for the third television season.

Our Radio Electronic Marketing Strategy

It was a challenge to get radio coverage for the Avalanche, with the Nuggets and Rockies having the major radio stations contracts. However, because of the competition among the large number of radio stations in the Denver area, we were able to negotiate a radio contract with a medium sized station, KLAK 1600 AM, for the inaugural season. We successfully attracted announcer Jack Jolly to do the play-by-play for fifteen games. Later, we were able to add Mike Ditchfield, who had joined us a Director of Player Development. Mike did the color commentary for us on our television games, which were cablecast by United Cable Systems and American Television & Communication Cablevision of Littleton, CO.

Marketing the Practice Facility at Mammoth Gardens

A scheduling problem developed while negotiating with McNichols Arena. The city could not provide us with practice time and space at the Arena. The complexity of physically redoing the arena floor almost daily to accommodate the Nuggets, Rockies and other entertainment events, made it impossible for the arena to provide practice time for us.

Luck again interceded on our behalf! We contacted a number of potential facilities close to our offices to determine if we could arrange for practices. Initially, we were unsuccessful! A few weeks later, we located a facility close to the arena, called Mammoth Gardens. Later, we nicknamed it our Mammoth "Garden of Eden." Mammoth Garden was a restaurant and bar that doubled as an entertainment and indoor sports facility. The restaurant area seated four hundred guests and offered a complete breakfast, lunch and dinner menu throughout the day, every day of the week.

Entertainment promoters, such as Barry Fey of Fey Productions, used Mammoth Gardens to host musical entertainment events and concerts. The floor was large enough to accommodate a practice field, but was made of concrete. We proposed to its management that we provide artificial turf carpeting over the concrete every time we practiced. They agreed to those conditions and we now had a practice facility used exclusively by us, complete with a mini arena and viewing seats.

We included Mammoth Gardens as one of our sponsors and co-marketed its facilities within our marketing materials. Additionally, Mammoth Gardens agreed to provide its facility to us for hosting Avalanche training parties. We invited our fan base to watch our practices and to play on the indoor turf when it was not used by the team. Afterwards, we served food and drink. All of these events helped us solidify our growing fan base. This became the first indoor soccer facility in Colorado for youth players

Figure 84
Future Avalanche Indoor Soccer Facility – 1982

Vertical Integration – Other Ancillary Revenue Petal Opportunities

One of the compelling marketing precepts I learned while working for I was to take the basic product we manufactured and spin off ancillary opportunities for generating revenue. I called this petal marketing and frequently used the same concept in later marketing endeavors. Today, sports franchises make as much money from ancillary revenue ideas as they do from ticket sales. Television was one example of how we implemented the concept of petal marketing. This marketing philosophy also led us to organize after-game events, which increased in-season ticket sales.

Jerry Kasten hired a staff of bright young marketers to develop additional petals of opportunities. We insisted on zero-based budgeting for most of these revenue ideas. Each petal had to pay for itself, whether from product sales or from funds contributed by our sponsors in support of the idea. These ancillary items included player-related merchandise with our logo, media guides, and day-of-game programs called the *Missile* magazine, souvenirs, such as key chains, hats and tee-shirts, bumper stickers, and our Avalanche summer day camp program for youth. Each idea provided additional revenue for the franchise.

The Magic Show – Day of Game

It is said that only the magician sees the magic! During the 1980s, the MISL was magic. The league was innovative in the way it presented its product. The ball was colored reddish orange so that it would bleed on television. Each team created its own magic show for its day-of-game event!

The Avalanche was to become one of the magicians, creating a fan entertainment environment that was second to none in the league. The league may have had owners that were self-made millionaires, but each team had professional marketers who seduced fans into coming to a game. Once there, the fans became enthralled and got caught up in the magic. The Avalanche had great marketers. Several advertisements ran in all the media, reinforcing the concept of "roars indoors" and "scream and shout." The game became a happing.

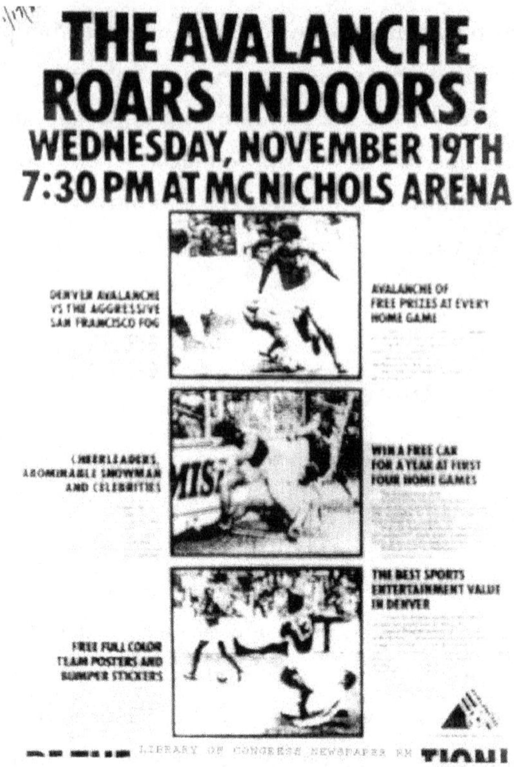

Figure 85
Advertisement
Avalanche Roars Indoors, Rocky Mountain News

In sports and in life, it's the follow-through that makes the difference. We now had a team and were training hard. Our public relations campaign was going strong. The media was generally supportive and the youth soccer associations were behind us. With all of this we had to produce. It came together on opening night of our first season. We needed to create an image that left the fans breathless and anxiously awaiting the next home game.

Planning the Magic Show

The day of a home game is very special in the life of a sports franchise, a time where everything comes together. We had been eagerly planning our inaugural home game since early summer and had put together a staff of about thirty people, both permanent and temporary, to assist us in crafting the magic show. We had created the "image" we wanted to portray to the fans and the media. Now, we had to pull together the myriad of day-of-game tasks required for every home game, and stir the pot, so that the final output was indeed a "Magic Show."

The detail involved in putting on a home game for any sporting event is mind boggling! Most of us who attend a sporting or entertainment event do not spend anytime wondering how it all happened. We are there to enjoy ourselves, and we expect to have a perfect and happy time doing so. The only time we think about any details is when something goes wrong.

Our job was to ensure that very little went wrong with our magic show. To make it even more difficult, with the exception of our Director of Administration, none of us had ever planned an event of this magnitude. Jerry Kasten and I did have some limited business experience at putting on sales meetings for several hundred people, but our business meeting experience paled when compared to putting on an Avalanche home game.

Every home game was controlled chaos! All the months of pre-planning came together in a three-hour event. Some of the major pre day-of-game tasks included creating marketing materials, generating public relations kits, persuading advertisers to buy advertisements, selling season and day-of-game tickets, generating a media guide, churning out a *Missile* Magazine Program, manufacturing the line of souvenirs, and ensuring we had inventory and vending staff to sell them at each game.

The league scheduled our first home game on Wednesday, November 19, 1980. The game was against another division rival, the San Francisco Fog. Their owners did not believe in staffing the team with American players and had predominantly foreign players on its roster. Interest was high among our owners since all but three of them were from the San Francisco bay area. It was a magical time in the history of the Avalanche. A dream was about to be realized.

Figure 86
Avalanche Opening Game
November 1980, Denver Avalanche

The Magic Begins

Imagine if you can, sitting in a luxurious and darkened indoor arena at game time waiting for your team to be introduced for the first time. The playing field is a plush, emerald green, fast-track surface. Suddenly, flashing strobe lights appear, swirling their multicolored beams around the arena. Then, deafening music starts playing! You feel your adrenalin rising and you are getting into the magic. Unexpectedly, a spotlight appears at one end of the arena. The light is focused on one of the goals, and it and the surrounding area is engulfed in artificial fog.

Unexpectedly, out of the fog and through the goal, strides the first of the Avalanche players, carrying a red rose like an Olympic torch! The noise cascades through the arena and the fans begin chanting "Avalanche! Avalanche! Avalanche!" The noise becomes louder and louder, then earsplitting, as each player is introduced by name and number.

The kids around the dasher boards are now wildly stomping their feet on the aluminum seats, the noise is roaring, crashing around you. The player calmly jogs over to the side of the field and presents a rose to a young female fan. The crowd goes crazy! Each player follows, also with a rose, and gives his rose to a young female fan.

This introduction became the signature opening of every home game. Never before had a sports team introduced its players with so much cool, style and magic. It was wondrous, and the fans loved it.

The lights were then turned up after this stirring introduction of the team. Usually, if you could again visualize yourself at the game, you would see the team begin its warm-up drills – not with our magic show! Instead, on the playing field, contrasted with the green Astroturf field, were two huge soccer balls about four feet high, brightly colored in orange and black. Unexpectedly, they began to turn slowly and gradually make their way down the field. Again, the crowd roared without restraint, mesmerized by the animated balls. "How does it work?" asks the fan next to you.

Suddenly, and again out of the goal, appear two look-a-like Disney characters. The Avalanche's version of "Goofy" was born. The two "Soccer Spaniel" characters proceeded to push the soccer balls even farther, propelling them into the goal. "Goooaaalll" bellowed through the loud speaker, churning the fans into frenzy! Suddenly, heads popped out of the balls, and our ball mascots and soccer spaniels are introduced! My youngest son, Craig, forever the entertainer, was now one of the team's mascots and became adored by young and old fans alike. He continued to "play to the crowd" for each of the Avalanche's home games, sometimes as a ball and sometimes as a soccer spaniel, helping us to reinforce our image as the "the magic show."

Abruptly, again coming onto the playing field from the opening in the goal, were our cheerleaders – all twenty-one of them! They were dressed in the team colors – short, green skirts, white and blue tops, and pompoms in green and blue. The Snow Cats then did a routine they had immortalized

125

while with the Denver Broncos. The fans chanted in repeated frenzy "Snow Cats! Snow Cats! Snow Cats!" Debbie La Porta, our Cheerleader Coordinator had the Snow Cats perform a routine that outdid anything they previously had performed for the Broncos. The Magic Show had begun, and now all could see, feel and hear the magic. Let the game begin!

The First Home Game

The Avalanche's first home game was played on Wednesday, November 19, 1980. We were initially disappointed with the league's scheduling of our first home game. It was sandwiched between the Nuggets and the Rockies games. We were also dissatisfied that we had been scheduled against the San Francisco Fog, one of the league's lowest-drawing teams. But, our San Francisco owners loved it.

We felt these two scheduling decisions gave us no marketing advantage. We had been hopeful that we would be pitted against one of the league's outstanding teams. It was not to be! In spite of the first game being against the Fog, we had 8,705 paid fans and 1,951 needy and disabled Art Reach fans for our first game. The Avalanche now roared. It was an exciting game. The arena reverberated with the sounds of "We Will Rock You." The Avalanche prevailed 4-3 in overtime, getting its first win. It had lost two previous away games to Buffalo and Cleveland, two of the stronger teams in the league. On a corner kick assist from Tony Graham, Marcelo Curi scored in just over three minutes of overtime. The song "Celebration" was to become the fan's song every time the Avalanche won.

The local Denver press and national soccer magazines were euphoric in their praise of the game. The *Rocky Mountain News,* said "An Avalanche of fun" is the MISL's selling point. The *Denver Post* headline was "Avalanche Eye Slice of Market" as they reported on the home opener. And, there were headlines written in the national magazine, *Soccer Corner,* about "The Game that kept the Fans Howling – MISL IS HERE TO STAY."

Figure 87
Chelo Curi Scoring the Winning Goal
Denver Avalanche

Fans reverberated that the game itself was a thrill-packed, high-powered and fast-paced winner. Clearly, the fans felt they were in touch with the expressions and emotions of the Avalanche players.

After-Game Fantasies

The marketing department had created a wonderful day-of-game event. Now that the Snow Cats were on board, it made even more sense. The staff contacted local restaurants to see if they would be interested in hosting an after-game party. All the potential restaurant locations approached had a dance floor and the capacity to handle a large crowd. Denver was one of the youngest cities in the United States. We strongly felt that the combination of our good-looking young players and cheerleaders would be a major attraction after a home game.

The arrangement made with each restaurant for each home game was simple. We would bring our players and cheerleaders to their restaurant after a game. They would provide food and drink for them. We agreed to advertise the restaurant in our day-of-game program magazine, the *Missile*. We had no idea if our home game party concept would prove successful, but we strongly felt that the chemistry would work. In retrospect, we had created a marketing monster.

All the staff members, the players and the Snow Cats would go to the advertised partner restaurant after the game. Those parties became the "in thing" to do in Denver and were huge. Some of our parties had over one thousand fans joining in the fun. We exceeded six hundred people at most of the after-game parties. This was to become a powerhouse method of building loyalty to the team.

The Avalanche was sold to the Tacoma Stars in 1983. I continued to play on men's adult teams until 1995. By then, two of my sons had finished their college education at Penn State. I got the opportunity to play with them and a number of other Cherry Creek Striker players who were now also college graduates. Few fathers get the opportunity to play on the same sports team with their sons. I was lucky and played on a men's soccer team soccer with my four sons and other youth players I had coached. What a thrill!"

Figure 88
Jeff Maierhofer at Penn State
By Ron Leonardi, Collegian Sports Writer
November 3, 1983

Figure 89
Cherry Creek Strikers
Maierhofer sons circa 1986
Tim, Jeff, Scott and Craig

The last men's team I played on in Denver was the Pepsi Rowdies over thirty men's team. I started playing with them in the late 80's and played into the 90's. It won the State of Colorado over thirty championship in 1993.

Figure 90
Pepsi Rowdies
Colorado State Champs
1993

Chapter 11
What Plays in Vegas Stays in Vegas – 1996

Early in 1996, I was providing strategic and marketing consulting in Denver to companies. A friend of mine, Bob Pesnik, was a consummate gambler. He mentioned he had just finished a book on Black Jack and wanted to test the principles laid out in his book. His problem was that he was barred from a number of Las Vegas Casino's because he was a card-counter. He also did not have the discipline for playing his system, which he described in detail in his book. He would play blackjack thirty hours at a time. He asked me if I would be willing to go to Vegas for a few months to play his system. He would guarantee any losses and pay a monthly consulting fee. I was single at the time and agreed to go to Vegas for a few months. That was without question, the strangest consulting job I have had in my life.

I drove from Denver to Vegas and settled in to play his system. As I remember, I gambled a small amount each bet, either $5.00 or $10.00 and over the course of the few months, played four times a day at various casinos'. I generally won over the few months I contracted to play his system.

Las Vegas, at the time, had a growing soccer program. They were playing all ages, youth, adult men and coed. I visited a field one Sunday and noticed two co-ed teams playing. I asked one of the players if they had a coach as I would be interested in playing for the exercise. I was quickly added to its coed team. Playing was pretty weird. Women on the team could not be charged or contact made with them. At the time, it really was not fulfilling but gave me an opportunity to play soccer on the weekend.

One of the male players on the team approached me and said he played on an over fifty men's team. Would I be interested in joining them? I responded quickly, looking forward to again playing soccer as I knew it. I was in shock when I showed up for the first practice. Most of the player's played college or professional soccer, either in the USA or other countries around the world. I only spent four months on the consulting project but playing with this team was a pure joy.

Chapter 12

The Old Dominion – Virginia
1997 – 2013

The Washington Dynamos 1999 – 2002

Shortly after returning to Denver from Las Vegas in 1996, I relocated to Springfield, Virginia in January of 1997, a part of the Washington, D.C. metro area. I had co-founded an internet information company and the majority of its prospects were in the Washington metropolitan area. Shortly after finding a place to live, I was able to locate a local 30+ men's team in Alexandria and played on it for a few years.

As luck would have it, I bumped into John Kerr, Sr. in 1999 at the La Canard restaurant in Vienna, VA. He was the Executive Director of the Major Soccer League Players Association at the time and had ties to the MISL. John mentioned he was playing on and managing a local over thirty team and asked if I would like to play on it. I said I would be thrilled. I joined the team as a young sixty-five-year-old. Little did I know at the time it would be the best amateur men's team on which I had ever played. It was even better than the Dallas Rangers and the Las Vegas over-forty-five team.

Figure 91
John Kerr, Sr.
Washington Dynamo 1999

John was the Dynamo's team manager, coach, and a player. John, born in Glasgow, Scotland, had an illustrious soccer career. He emigrated from Scotland to Canada and played on the Canadian national team from 1968 to 1977. He had played throughout that time period for several NASL teams, including the Cosmos and the Washington Diplomats. He played for the Cosmos from 1972 to 1976, which had world-renowned teammates like Pele of Brazil, Chinaglia of Italy and Werner Roth of Germany. Later, he joined the Washington Diplomats in 1976. John was inducted into the Virginia-Washington D.C. Soccer Hall of Fame in 2008. I remember his induction ceremony in Richmond, VA.

Figure 92
John Kerr, Sr.
Induction into
Virginia Athletic Hall of Fame
Richmond, VA 2008

While playing for the Diplomats in 1976, his teammate was Carl Minor. Carl, born in Austria, played center forward for Westhampton in the English Premier League. He later played in the NASL for several teams from 1973-1977. Carl played center midfield for us on the Dynamo.

Figure 93
Carl Minor
NASL Diplomats 1975-76

I was surprised when I first saw Dave Butler was also on the Dynamo. Dave had played in the NASL for the Seattle Sounders and Portland Timber from 1974-1978. Later, he played in the MISL for the Baltimore Blast, Kansas City Comets and Philadelphia Fever from 1979 to 1983.

Figure 94
Dave Butler
NASL and MISL

Our center back on the team was George Lidster. At that time, George was the coach of George Washington University. He held that coaching position from 1987 to 2011. His teams had 191 wins while he was the coach. George was from Durham, England and immigrated to the United States to play soccer at the University of Illinois, Springfield. While at the university, George became an All-American. In 1986, he, Jonny Kerr, Bruce Murray, Bruce Stolmeyer and Desmond Armstrong all played on the Fairfax Spartans, which won the 1986 National Amateur Cup Championship. George was later to become involved with me in several soccer activities. He retired in 2011 and moved with his wife Valerie to Pawley's Island, SC, where he was the Technical Director of Beach S.C. Years after we played together in Northern Virginia, we hooked up again in South Carolina. Pawley's Island is about a 35-40 minute drive from my home in North Myrtle Beach.

Figure 95
George Lidster
Coach George Washington University

Our center forward on the team was Bobby Iskenov. He was a fabulous player. I was told he played on the Bulgaria World Cup Team. I don't recall any other information about him except that he was a magician in the penalty area and could score goals.

Rich Shelton was our playmaker and at the time one of the outstanding players on the team. He played professional soccer in England at a young age and immigrated to the United States to attend college. He was a four year All-American at Mercyhurst College in Pennsylvania. He was a member of the Regional ODP program in Pennsylvania and was a player-coach on the USISL Kalamazoo Kingdom, 1999-2002, which was in the development league for the MLS. Rich had EUFA and USSF "B" licenses. Rich currently is the President and Technical Director of the Reston Soccer Club, which has about 1500 children in both recreational and travel soccer.

Figure 96
Rich Shelton – Washington Dynamo
Director, Herndon Soccer Association

Trevor Parker played left midfield on the team and was a brilliant player. Born in England, he played for several professional clubs, including Tottenham Hotspurs of the English Premier League. He had over 200 goals as a professional. Trevor came to the United States in the mid-1990s and was first associated with Britannia, one of the largest youth soccer camp company's at the time. He is currently the Director of Coaching for Annandale United Soccer Club, which many of you may remember as the Annandale Boys and Girls Club. Prior to that, he was the Assistant Technical Director of highly ranked McLean Soccer Association. He has a USSF "A" coaching license and a European "A" license. Teams he has coached have won numerous Virginia State Championships. Trevor also was a D.C United staff coach. Trevor and I have been business partners since 2003.

Figure 97
Trevor Parker – Washington Dynamo
Director of Coaching
Annandale United Soccer Club

Figure 98
German Hungarians 1997
Alumni Exhibition Game

Figure 99
Jeff Maierhofer 1997
German Hungarian Alumni Game

Northern Virginia Youth Soccer 1997-2014

During those early years in Northern Virginia, I coached and trained for various competitive/travel teams in the Washington Area Girls Soccer (WAGS) League, National Capital Soccer League (NCSL) and Old Dominion Soccer League (ODSL).

The first youth team I coached was part of The Lee Mount Vernon Soccer Association, located in located in Alexandria, VA. I had solidified my work activities and was playing with the Dynamos, an over-forty-five men's team. I wanted to get back into coaching youth soccer. I was engaged to Sandra Lee Ferony at the time and we shared a townhouse in Kingstowne, a community within Alexandria, VA.

Sandra suggested that I advertise as a personal coach offering to train youth soccer players one-on-one. I ran an ad in a local newspaper in late 2001. The first response to the ad was from Lee Emery, a neighbor living close to us. He mentioned he had a daughter playing soccer and he wanted to help develop her skills. Would I be interested in training her, one on one at the local recreation center outdoor field next to their home? His daughter's name was Kate and I agreed to train her.

It started raining during one of the late afternoon training sessions. Since Kate lived next to the field, I escorted her home. She was unable to get in the house and her parents were working. I suggested she come home with me until her parents arrived later that afternoon. I explained to her that Sandra and her daughter Sharon, a teacher, were at the house. She agreed and came back to the house with me. Later, her parents arrived home and picked her up. That evening, Lee called me and suggested I not train Kate again since it was just the two of us and anything could happen. I agreed and learned a lesson about training youth one-on-one.

The next day, Lee called me and shocked me. Since I had done an outstanding job with his daughter, he wanted to know if I be interested in training her travel team, which played in the Lee Mount Vernon Soccer League. The team, named the Stars n Stripes, had been looking for a new coach for the spring 2002 season. I met with the parents of the team and they asked if I would coach their children. I quickly agreed to coach them. It was a wonderful experience and I trained and coached the team for two seasons.

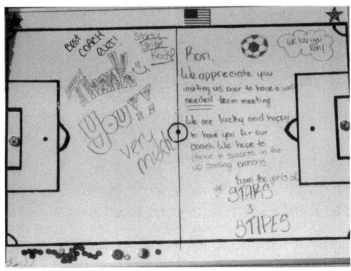

Figure 100
Stars n Stripes
Girls Soccer Team 2003

I received a call from Lula Bauer in 2003. She was the Executive Director of the Lee Mount Vernon Soccer Association. She asked me if I would be interested in training its coaches on the Principles of Team Play. I told her I would be delighted and spent several weeks training its coaches. Said Lula Bauer after I gave the coaching course "I have had the pleasure of sitting in on Ron Maierhofer's coaching course. I am certain coaches that attended felt equipped to further develop their players. After all, that's what it's all about, isn't it? Development! Two thumbs up!" Lula has had an outstanding soccer administrative and coaching career since those early days.

Figure 101
Lula Bauer
Lee Mount Vernon Soccer Association
2001-2018

Sports Education and Training, LLC 2002 -2007

Sports Education and Training International, LLC. (**SETI**) was a holding company co-founded by me in 2002 as a Virginia Limited Liability Company. It then formed CornerKick Soccer Education and Training, L.L.C. (CSET) to carry out its business strategy. Entities formed by CSET included CornerKick Goal,

LLC, Cornerkick Soccer Camps, LLC, CornerKick Properties, LLC and CornerKick Soccer Academy, LLC. The concept required attracting a number of qualified partners who could carry out SETI's strategies.

SETI was an early entry soccer-focused education technology and training company providing eLearning and DVD based instructional materials for soccer players and coaches. It marketed to sports and fitness centers, sports arenas, schools, community organizations, childcare centers, and youth associations, teams and leagues that manage and provide athletic opportunities to youth. It delivered educational training through various multi-media platforms. SETI required a number of additional partners to help implement its strategic concepts.

I set about to interest several potential partners in the concept. The first to be contacted was Frank Cuzzi, a classmate and fraternity brother of mine at Cornell. Frank had a company in New York City called Corner Kick International, Inc. and he also owned the Cornerkick trademark.

Frank, although never having played soccer, was heavily involved in our sport and was a consultant to a number of soccer entities. He previously had been the Director of Advertising and Marketing for the North American Soccer League (NASL) and the Director of Marketing for the Major Indoor Soccer League (MISL). He became our President of CK Properties.

Figure 102
Cornerkick Logo 2002

Frank mentioned that John Webster, another classmate of ours at Cornell, had recently sold his management search company located in New York City and was looking for an investment. John and I were teammates on Cornell's lacrosse team and later met to discuss the SETI concept. He had a strong background in securities, financial, and senior management. John also decided to be part of the founding members of SETI and became President of CornerKick Soccer Education and Training, LLC, its operating company.

The team was in need of a sports-related general counsel. Sandra Ferony, then my fiancé, worked at Greenberg Traurig PC, one of the outstanding law firms in Northern Virginia. Its Managing General Partner was Tom Hicks, who is a wonderful vocalist. He and Sandra sang at local restaurants in Northern Virginia and Sandra was able to convince Tom to chat with me. Tom was excited about the SETI opportunity and agreed to come aboard as general counsel.

Trevor Parker who played with me on the Dynamos was also interested. One of our main challenges when forming SETI was to recruit an outstanding, highly regarded partner as its technical advisor for soccer. Trevor fitted the bill. He had a EUFA "B" Coaching license (now an "A" USSF license) and had played for the Tottenham Hotspurs in the English Premier League. He also had been an executive in the late 90s with Britannia, one of the largest camp operations in the United States. Trevor agreed to join the company and became President of CK Soccer Academy, LLC. We have been business partners for the last sixteen years in SETI's successor, Soccer Club Management, LLC.

One of the markets we were looking to expand into was eLearning. Dave Pistell owned the G.O.A.L. Trademark. I helped Dave coach his youth team earlier and knew about the trademark. He had an eLearning, marketing, and business development background. Dave agreed to join the company. In return for letting the company use the G.O.A.L. trademark, Dave agreed to an equity position in SETI. He became our President of CornerKick Soccer Camps, LLC. I became the President of CornerKick Goal, LLC, and SETI's eLearning entity. We filled out the partnership team by adding Richard Broad and Dave Ungrady to CSET.

Dave Ungrady joined our partnership team as the Vice President of Development of CSET. Dave played soccer through high school at Notre Dame H.S. and was named to the Virginia High School Soccer Hall of Fame. He attended the University of Maryland and played on its varsity soccer team. Dave was inducted into the Notre Dame H.S. Athletic Hall of Fame. He also played for the Virginia Royals, a minor soccer league.

Dave wrote a book "Unlucky" about his struggles in the minor leagues. He was the Editor of the Virginia Youth Soccer Association's magazine "Touchline." Dave has been a broadcaster for ESPN, CNN, Voice of America and the FIFA World Cup broadcasts. He has since written two more books. Dave is a terrific marketer.

Richard Broad also joined CSET as its Executive Vice President. Richard had a wonderful soccer background. He played at Princeton University and received his Master's in Education from the University of Massachusetts. He served as an assistant coach at both schools. Richard was the head coach of George Mason University from 1976-1984 and at the time was President of Middle States Soccer Camps.

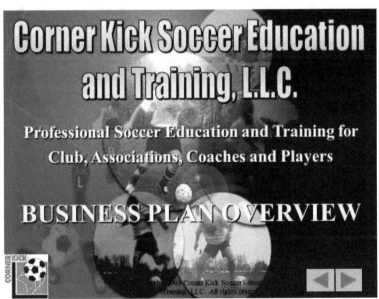

Figure 103
CSET Business Plan - 2002

Figure 104
CSET Organization Chart - 2002

Our executive staff was complete and we began operations in 2002. Shortly after we formed the SETI companies, we were approached by London based Soccer Tutor. Soccer Tutor was then interested in partnering with us to develop sales for them in the United States. Its product was animated soccer drills. Soccer Tudor has since become one the leading companies in that field. We negotiated a strategic partnership with Soccer Tudor and were at the contract-signing stage.

Before signing the documents, we reviewed our strategic mission and felt that we would be better suited to develop our own animated soccer drills and practice plans. We notified Soccer Tudor that we would not be moving forward with the strategic partnership. It took us almost a year to create hundreds of online soccer drills using animation, online practice plans for all age groups, and three DVDs, *Move and Fakes to Beat a Defender (Beginner, Intermediate and Advanced)*. The DVDs used animation, voice over, text, and video. These intellectual assets still exist today.

Once we completed the design and creation of these online products, we began marketing them through CSET. It was an early-entry marketer of online soccer drills and practice plans.

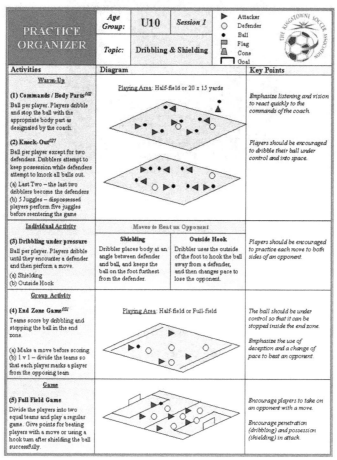

Figure 105
CSET Online Practice Plan
2004

SETI and CSET were operational until 2005. Several of the original co-founders of SETI founded Soccer Club Management, LLC (SCM) in 2009 and still operational in 2018. Those founders were Trevor Parker, Tom Hicks, Jonny Taylor and myself. The intellectual assets created by CSET are still being used today.

Figure 106
Moves and Fakes to Beat a Defender
Beginner 2005

High School Coaching 2004-2007

The former member of CSET' executive staff was Richard Broad. Richard was coaching Fairfax County's Woodson H.S. Varsity Boys Team in 2004. He asked me if I would be interested in coaching the Girls Junior Varsity Team. I agreed to help him out. At the end of the 2004 season, Richard asked me to be his assistant with the Boys' Varsity Team in 2005 to which I also agreed. The Woodson Cavalier's Soccer Team went 17-4-1 that year and went to the Virginia State Title and lost.

Richard was also a soccer analyst for CBS College Sports. He was inducted into the VA-DC Soccer Hall of Fame in 2016. George Mason University inducted him into its Hall of Fame in 2008. He is the President of American

Soccer Programs and for many years, was the President of Middle States Soccer

Figure 107
Richard Broad
Big Ten Color Commentator
Big Ten Network

Brent Leiba approached me in 2006 and said he had just been named Head Coach of boys' varsity team at Lee High School, Springfield VA. He asked if I would like to be his assistant and I agreed. Brent had played for the George Mason University Patriots for four years and graduated in 2001. This was to be his first head coaching job. He did a terrific job with Lee High School and Brent is the current head coach of Howard University and has been its head coach since 2008. Brent also has been on the coaching staff of the Washington Freedom Professional Team since 2001.

Figure 108
Brent Leiba – Head Coach
Howard University 2008–2018

While at Lee High School, Brent managed to also add Clyde Watson as a technical assistant. Clyde was the Assistant Head Coach of the Washington Freedom Professional Women's Team. Through the years he helped coach U.S. National Team Players like Mia Ham, Abby Wambach, Brandy Chastain, Julie Foudy, Cat Whitehill and Ali Krieger.

Clyde was born in Guyana and played 10 years on the Guyana National Team. He immigrated to the USA and played collegiate soccer at Clemson University. I knew of Clyde from his days playing indoor soccer. Our Avalanche team played against him when he was a player for the Philadelphia Fever and Wichita Wings. He played in the MISL from 1979-82. The National Soccer Coaches Association of America (NSCAA) named him its Youth Coach of the Year in 2007.

Clyde has been the Technical Director of McLean Soccer Association since 2007. My business partner Trevor Parker, was the Director of Coaching with Clyde before leaving to join the Annandale United Soccer Club. When Clyde assisted us with the technical development of the Lee H.S. boys' varsity soccer team, he was pure genius as a coach. I do not believe I have seen or worked with anyone as good. I learned more from watching Clyde train at Lee H.S. than I had from anyone previously.

Figure 109
Clyde Watson, 2018
Washington Freedom Assistant Coach

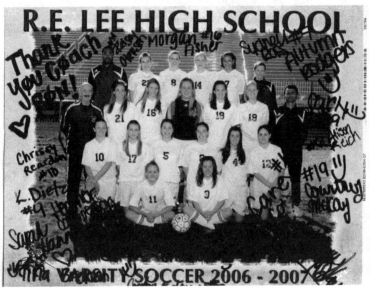

Figure 110
Lee H.S. School Varsity Soccer Team
2006-2007

KinderKickIt 2004-2018

Figure 111
KinderKickIt
George Mason University
2007

Kingstowne Soccer Association 2007 – 2018

I had lived in Kingstowne, VA since I arrived at Northern Virginia in 1997. Kingstowne was a newer community within the historic city of Alexandria. Previously, I had provided individual one on one coaching and several group training programs to the Kingstowne Recreation Center. Since living in Kingstowne, I had coached teams that were members of associations throughout Northern Virginia, including Alexandria, Vienna, Ashburn, Sterling, Centreville, Hayfield, and Leesburg. Coaching teams in these associations required a significant amount of weekly travel.

I decided to organize a soccer association for the municipality of Kingstowne, Virginia and its surrounding area residents. I wanted the association to promote participation in the game of soccer and teach the principles of soccer excellence, sportsmanship, athletic skills, team spirit, character and social interaction. Its goals would be to emphasize the ideals of enjoyment, fair play, safety, integrity, and honesty, through age and ability-appropriate competition. It would provide soccer educational opportunities and enable every member of KSA to achieve their personal goals. The coaches would be professionals and not parents and the children would be offered exciting soccer enrichment programs, whether recreational or competitive.

I wrote the application for a 501(c)(3) association in March of 2007. It was approved several months later and we began operations in September 2007. A number of professional coaches were interested in joining us and we started the club with over thirty local professional coaches. I was fortunate to attract Scott Racek who became our Director of Coaching.

Figure 112
Scott Racek - Coach Edison H.S.
And Kingstowne Soccer Association 2007

Scott coached soccer at Edison High School located close to Kingstowne. We began operations with ten teams ages five to eighteen. One of the players who played on the Edison High School team and for us was Andy Najar. Andy later became the MLS Rookie of the Year in 2009 and a member of the Honduras National Team in 2018.

Figure 113
Andy Najar – Edison H.S. and D.C. United
MLS Rookie of the Year 2009
Honduras National Team 2018
Kingstowne Soccer Association

By 2008 the association was established and growing. My business commitments prevented me from spending the time required to lead the association. I asked Scott if he would take over as President and the board, by acclamation, voted him President. I remained its Chairman through the years. The association is still active.

Soccer Club Management, LLC 2009-2018

Soccer Club Management, LLC (SCM), the successor to Sports Education and Technology, LLC, was formed in 2009 by me, Trevor Parker, Tom Hicks, Esq. and Jonny Taylor. I merged my KinderKickIt operations into SCM when it was founded. The founders have a combination of backgrounds in content, sports management, soccer training and education, distance & eLearning, corporate law, and technology, coupled with the Internet business development experience related to the affinity social community.

SCM is a sports-focused education technology holding company providing educational training for athletes and coaches in soccer. It provides eLearning and live instructional training for players and coaches in a variety of soccer settings. It markets to schools, childcare centers, sports clubs, fitness centers, county, state and federal governments, corporations, leagues, associations, teams, coaches, communities, and sports arenas that manage and provide soccer athletic opportunities to youth.

It currently delivers soccer educational training live and through various multi-media platforms, including online and dvds. It also provides on-site youth soccer enrichment programs under the KinderKickIt', CornerKickIt' and Touch and Technique™ brands.

Figure 114
KinderKickIt T-Shirt Example

The company's soccer enrichment programs have been created to provide year-round youth soccer enrichment activities targeted at the childcare and youth training markets. The programs are turnkey or customized and are usually six weeks in length. The programs are normally paid for by the parents as an optional activity.

One of its strategies is to offer sport & health clubs and indoor soccer facilities a three-pronged training program that enables them to be competitive with local youth associations. These target clients are able to differentiate by applying the eLearning content to the reinforcement of live training. As an example, the company received a two-year contract with Sport & Health, Inc., a major regional sport and health fitness company in Northern Virginia. It has approximately thirty-five clubs. The company provided in-house soccer training to the children of its members.

Figure 115
KinderKickIt Flyer

The Company has developed soccer eLearning and streaming video content, which contains hundreds of drills and activities for players and trainers. Its content can be downloaded onto personal devices and other media platforms. The content is easily converted to any private label. Its eLearning content is available to users through controlled access by using identification and password technology. Content is produced in several media including video, animation, voice-over, and text. Its technology was developed in 2003 by SETI, the company's predecessor. The Company has operations in Virginia, Maryland, Washington DC, Minnesota, and South Carolina.

Chapter 13
On the Beach in Myrtle Beach
2014 – Present

Sandra and I decided to semi-retire in 2014. We had become shag dancers in 1997 and over the years attended many shag events in North Myrtle Beach, SC. Shag dancing, a form of swing dancing, is the state dance of South Carolina. North Myrtle Beach is part of the Grand Strand, an area covering approximately sixty miles of coastal beaches from the South Carolina's northern border to Georgetown, SC. The Myrtle Beach/North Myrtle Beach area attracts over seventeen million visitors a year and is milder in the winter than northern cities and cooler in the summer than Southern Florida. North and South Carolina market to older demographics and make the states attractive to retirees.

We visited North Myrtle Beach in early 2014 to find housing. We located a perfect house in a community called Barefoot Resort and Golf, which is three minutes from the ocean. Sandra and I share eight children and nineteen grandchildren and anticipated many of them visiting us. We sold our home in

Figure 116
My Wife
Sandra Ferony Maierhofer

Northern Virginia in twelve days and in September of 2014 relocated to North Myrtle Beach. Trevor Parker is still operating our company, Soccer Club Management, LLC, from Vienna, VA.

I am still involved with Soccer Club Management, contributing marketing, financial and tax consulting to the company. One day, shortly after we settled in the community, I noticed a young coach training a high school age boy. I stopped and introduced myself. The coach was Robert Bass and he had a significant soccer background. He played in college and was a travel coach for Coast FA, the largest soccer association on the Grand Strand. Robert is a member of the Myrtle Beach Mutiny, a professional soccer team playing in the Professional Development League (PDL). I asked Robert if he was interested in learning about KinderKickIt and after hearing my short summary of the company, said he would be very interested in coming aboard. We hired him in late 2014 as our Regional Director and started our South Carolina soccer operations.

Since that time, Robert and his staff have contributed to building our South Carolina activities. The company, in the spring of 2015, was presented an opportunity with the City of North Myrtle Beach's Parks and Recreation Department (NMB Rec). The city has approximately three hundred participants in its recreational program. Robert asked me if I would handle the opportunity and I agreed.

I met with Matt Decker, its Assistant Athletic Director and we formed a strategic partnership with them by the end of the meeting. We kicked off our new partnership in the spring of 2015 with a program for three- to eight-year-old kids. Eighty-five kids signed up. We have continually provided programs to the city since 2015.

Matt Decker called me in August of 2015 and asked if I was interested in heading up the tryouts and the team selection process for its fall 2015 league program? I answered yes and oversaw the team selection process for two seasons. Matt called again after the 2016 fall season and asked if I would coach its U9 all-star team that was to compete in the State Recreational Parks championship. I selected the all-stars for the team and coached it to the semi-finals of the state championship.

Prior to the 2017 NMB Parks and Rec spring program, Matt was promoted to its Athletic Director. He asked me if I would write a coaches' training manual for all age groups. I agreed and provided him with a coaching manual for all his recreational coaches. Also in 2017, Soccer Club Management became a strategic partner with the Coast FA Soccer Association, providing programs for its 3-5-year-old players. We provide it coaches and programs under our KinderKickIt brand.

What dream is next?

Writing this book has pleasantly taken me back through my soccer life. And what a journey it has been! Often, the bumpy parts of the road as one goes through life, are mostly forgotten or buried deep in one's mind. The beauty of the human mind is that it often remembers the good times or isolated parts of an experience.

To refresh my frequent and unforgiving loss of memory, I have used the Internet, conversations with friends and teammates who shared similar experiences, and my computer files. I was shocked to see that over the years, I had created over 315,000 computer files, many of which are related to my soccer journey. Those soccer computer files, when referenced, brought back memories, which helped me recreate parts of this journey.

I have highlighted my nomadic soccer journey as it has taken its many forks in the road. As is always the case with life's forks in the road, we make decisions based on our personal, business or family issues at the time. I have no remorse about decisions made. Rather than reminisce about the past, I find myself thinking of new ideas, a different twist on my current soccer activities, or a potential new soccer venture.

As I captured in my earlier book about the Denver Avalanche Major Indoor Soccer Team, "imagine if you can, sitting in a luxurious and darkened indoor arena at game time waiting for your team to be introduced for the first time. The playing field is a plush, emerald green, fast-track surface. Suddenly, flashing strobe lights appear, swirling their multicolored beams around the arena. Then, deafening music starts playing! You feel your adrenalin rising and you are getting into the magic. Unexpectedly, a spotlight appears at one end of the arena. The light is focused on one of the goals, and it and the surrounding area is engulfed in artificial fog… **It's game time!** As I reflect on my soccer journey, I convince myself I am ready for another game! I hope you have enjoyed my journey. I await another soccer dream!

Description of Figures

Many of the figures below, with the exception of figures attributed as noted, are taken directly from the Denver Avalanche's marketing materials. These materials include, but are not limited to, the Denver Avalanche Media Guides for the 1980-82 seasons, the Denver Avalanche *Missile* Magazines, the Denver Avalanche logo, programs, schedules, ticket plans, business plans, photographs, advertisements, demographic study, and likenesses of merchandise and uniforms. During its 1980-1983 history, the Denver Avalanche received permissions to use photographs and images of those individuals shown in the figures.

FIGURE # - NAME

1. Coach Ron at Seventy-Five Years of Age
2. The Author, circa 2016
3. No Money Down How to Buy a Sports Franchise
4. Len Oliver Soccer Hall of Fame
5. Germania Soccer Club 1932
6. Eddie Maierhofer circa 1932
7. Germania Soccer Club Old Photo Album
8. Bertha Maierhofer, Mom
9. Ron 1935
10. Maierhofer Truck 1951 Ron Accident to Bumper
11. Ron and Howie 1941
12. Howie and Ron 1942
13. Our Soccer Team 1948 The Old Swimming Hole

14. Maierhofer Meat's Youth Team 1949
15. 1951 Buffalo Beck's Reserve Team
16. Eintracht Frankfurt Futball Team Logo
17. Ron and Rudy Berger 1951
18. Hans (John) Felgemacher
19. Park School Athletic Hall of Fame
20. Soldier of the Month 1955
21. Norm Weidner circa 2000
22. Huntington L.I. NY 1956
23. Howie article U.S. Olympic Team 1956
24. Legendary Penn State Coach Bill Jeffries
25. Coach Herb Mols 1975 NY State Empire Games
26. Cornell Soccer Team 1958
27. Clive Beckford Memorial Award 1959
28. Bob Kane Article 1960
29. U.S. National Soccer Team 1959
30. Dan Wood, Coach of Cornell/Caribous NASL
31. Bruce Arena Cornell Hall of Fame 1986
32. Ron Maierhofer Cornell Hall of Fame 1986
33. Cornell Hall of Fame Ceremony Sept.19, 1986. Sons Jeff, Tim, Ron, Scott, Craig
34. Dave Sarachan National Team Coach 2017
35. All Ivy Team 1959
36. All American Team 1959
37. U.S. Soccer Hall of Fame Brick
38. Harry S. Truman Fireside Chat, April 18, 1960
39. President, Alumni Class 1960 Cornell
40. United States Olympic Book 1960
41. George Brown U.S. National Team 1959
42. Ron and Miss USA 1959
43. Alex Ely U.S. National Team 1959
44. 1959 U.S. National Soccer Team Relaxing
45. Cincinnati Kolping Logo

46. L.A. Maccabi's 1070's

47. Hans Gudegast/Eric Braeden

48. Al Zerhusan L.A. Kickers 1960's

49. Joe Eschell Dallas Tornado 1969-74

50. Neil Cohen – Denver Avalanche

51. Dallas Tornado NASL Champions 1973

52. Dallas Tornado NASL Champions 1974

53. Kyle Rote, Sr. New York Giants - NFL

54. Kyle Rote, Jr. NASL 1974

55. JJ Pearce H.S. Assistant Coach 1971. Photo by Pearce H.S. Alumni Sports Banquet

56. JJ Pearce H.S. Assistant Coach 1973-74

57. Richardson Soccer League 1971

58. North Texas All-Stars Selection 1975

59. Rob Harper Memorial 2014

60. Start of Richardson Sparta Soccer Club

61. Sparta Selection of Coaches 1975

62. National "B" License 1976

63. National "C" License 1976

64. Photo Bronze Statute of Pele 1978

65. Finished Bronze Statute of Pele 1978

66. MISL Brochure Cover 1980

67. McNichols Arena Denver 1980-81

68. Howard Maierhofer Avalanche Owner

69. Stan Musial and St. Louis Steamers 1980

70. MISL Game 1980

71. Earl "The Pearl" Monroe 1980

72. Avalanche Staff Directory 1980-81

73. Winner Name the Team Contest 1980

74. Avalanche Logo 1980

75. Avalanche Ad Scream and Shout 1980

76. Game Demographics 1980

77. Children's World Schedule 1980

78.   As Avalanche Roars Indoors 1980
79.   Avalanche Cheerleader Coordinator 1980
80.   Avalanche Cheerleaders 1980
81.   Ad Budweiser 1980
82.   Missile Magazine – Buffalo Stallions 1980
83.   Avalanche TV Staff 1980-81
84.   Future Avalanche Indoor Facility 1982
85.   Avalanche Ad Roars Indoors 1980
86.   Avalanche Opening Game 1980
87.   Chelo Curi Scoring Winning Goal 1981
88.   Jeff Maierhofer at Penn State by Ron Leonardi. Collegian Sports Writer, Nov. 3, 1983
89.   Sons Tim, Jeff, Scott and Craig 1986
90.   Pepsi Rowdies Colorado State Champs 1903
91.   John Kerr, Sr. 1999
92.   John Kerr, Sr. Northern VA Hall of Fame 2008
93.   Carl Minor – NASL Diplomats 1975-76
94.   Dave Butler – NASL and MISL
95.   George Lidster Coach GW University
96.   Rich Shelton Director Herndon Soccer Assoc.
97.   Trevor Parker Director of Coaching Annandale
98.   German Hungarian Alumni Game 1997
99.   Jeff Maierhofer German Hungarian Game 1997
100. Stars n Stripe Girls Soccer Team 2003
101. Lula Bauer Lee Mount Vernon Soccer Assoc.
102. CornerKickIt Logo 2002
103. CSET Business Plan 2002
104. CSET Organization Chart 2002
105. CSET Online Practice Plan 2004
106. Move and Fakes to Beat a Defender DVD 2003
107. Richard Broad Big Ten Color Commentator
108. Brent Leiba Head Coach Howard University
109. Clyde Watson Coach Washington Freedom

NOTES – 1
The Author Played in Nineteen States

California 1963-1968

Colorado 1976-1995

Connecticut 1957-1960

Illinois 1953, 1959

Indiana 1959

Maine 1957-1960

Maryland 2001-2002

Massachusetts 1957-1960

Michigan 1954

Missouri 1959

Nevada 1996

New Hampshire 1957-1960

New Jersey 1957-1960

New Mexico 1987

New York 1942-55, 1961-62, 2003

Ohio 1962, 1968-1971

Pennsylvania 1957-1960, 1997

Texas 1971-1975

Virginia 1997-2002

NOTES – 2
The Author Played in Forty Two Cities

Albuquerque, NM, Buffalo, NY, Cheyenne, WY,
Chicago, IL, Cincinnati, OH, Cleveland, OH, Dallas, TX,
Dayton, OH, Denver, CO, Detroit, MI, District of Columbia
Flushing Heights, NY, Franklyn Square, NY. Ft. Erie, Ontario,
Canada, Glen Cove, NY, Great Neck, NY, Hamilton, Ontario,
Canada, Harmorville, PA, Hempstead, NY, Houston, TX
Huntington, NY, Indianapolis, IN, Ithaca, NY
Jamestown, NY, Kitchener, Ontario, Canada,
Lindenhurst, NY, London, Ontario, Canada, Los Angeles, CA
Massapequa, NY, Mineola, NY, Niagara Falls, NY
Niagara Falls, Ontario, Canada Richardson, TX, Rochester, NY
Providence, RI. St. Catharine, Ontario, Canada, St. Louis, Missouri
Sea Cliff, NY, Snyder, NY, Toronto, Ontario, Canada
Welland, Ontario, Canada, Windsor, Ontario, Canada

NOTES – 3
The Author Played for the United States against Six Countries

United States vs Argentina Lost 4-1
United States vs Brazil Won 5-3
United States vs Costa Rica Lost 4-3
United States vs Cuba Won 5-0
United States vs Haiti Won 7-2
United States vs Mexico Won 4-2

NOTES – 4
The Author Coached in Six States

Colorado
Ohio
New York
South Carolina
Texas
Virginia

NOTES – 5
The Author Started Entities which Play or Played in 14 States

Arizona, California, Colorado, Connecticut
Kansas, Illinois, Maryland, Minnesota
Missouri, Pennsylvania, San Francisco
South Carolina, Texas, Virginia

CPSIA information can be obtained
at www.ICGtesting.com
Printed in the USA
BVHW041144261121
622595BV00019B/386